· 美国语文拓展阅读系列 ·
英汉对照插图版 英语辅学经典

妙语名篇

Witticisms and Famous Articles

心灵的塑造

尹燕燕 / 主编

北京联合出版公司
Beijing United Publishing Co.,Ltd.

使 用 说 明

心灵成长，素质教育
选文充满哲理，对坚强内心的培养有着积极的意义，于无声处滋养心灵的成长，让人全面倍增正能量。

精美插图，丰富多彩
书中近百幅精美插图，让读者在享受美文阅读的同时，欣赏世界绘画大师的佳作。

地道英文，原汁原味
本书入选篇目均为英语经典美文，语言准确、地道。

选材丰富，贴近生活
书中收录数十篇与日常生活紧密相关的美文，内容涉及亲情、友情，感恩、信念，成长、改变，哲思、智慧等多个方面。

USER'S GUIDE

名言寄语，经典励志
本书精选西方各领域名人
语录五十余则，不仅能让
读者领略西方大家们的风
采，更主要的是学会很多
做人的道理。

单词短语，一网打尽
每篇文章后面附有中学生
考试必备单词、实战短
语，将美文阅读与英语学
习相结合。

妙语
名篇 ✦ *Witticism and Famous Articles*
幸福的本质

There, in the hospital emergency room, I held her hand and we had
a moment together. Because she had taught me that it was important to
be able to laugh at any circumstance and at myself. And of course, to
always wear clean underwear!

She *squeezed* my hand and rested.

Everything was going to be all right.

After all, she knew she had on clean underwear.

人是自己幸福的设计者。

——H. D. 梭罗

19岁那年的一天下午，父亲打电话给我，说他在医院急救室。他和
母亲出了车祸，两人都无大碍，就母亲受了点伤。

我们进车，冲进了医院：母亲躺在轮床上，护士正拿着敷布按在她
额头上。她是从挡风玻璃摔出来的，划断了脸上的动脉。母亲的脸到处
是血，看起来很恐怖，其他部位没什么问题。

她看着我，似乎想寻求安慰。

猛然间，我知道该怎么做了。我俯身贴近她的耳朵，小声说道：
"您穿的是干净的内裤吗？"

/ 62

单词记忆

experience [ɪkˈspɪərɪəns] v. 经历, 体验, 感受

例：We learn from the past, experience the present and hope for
success in the future.

我们从过去中学习，体验现在，展望未来的成功。

profound [prəˈfaʊnd] adj. 深奥的, 极度的, 意义深远的

例：We all have profound admiration and respect for him.

我们都深常钦佩和尊敬他。

responsibility [rɪˌspɒnsɪˈbɪlɪtɪ] n. 责任, 职责, 责任心

例：Our teacher has a high sense of responsibility.

我们老师有高度的责任感。

短语指排

It depends on what you mean ...

depend on: 依靠; 依赖

造：_____

I added up my little moments of pleasure yesterday.

add up: 合计

造：_____

译席参考

对于成年人来说，幸福是复杂的。

译：_____

幸福不是凭空产生，而是亲身觉得有。

译：_____

过一种宁静中庸的生活
To Lead a Quiet Life 47

经典译文，准确流畅
在每篇英语文章之后，都附有
汉语译文，帮助读者准确理解
文章的内容。

翻译测试，全面提升
每篇文章后面附有翻译测
试题，有利于提高读者的
翻译和习作水平。

前言
PREFACE

　　你想学好英语吗？你想了解西方人的生活情趣和内心世界吗？你想避免有朝一日遇见外国人跟你打招呼，却因你英语水平太低而难于启齿的尴尬吗？一连串的问题摆在我们面前，犹如当头棒喝，值得每一个人去思考，尤其是充满理想和抱负的学生们。

　　可能现在的你正为英语考试而犯愁，一部部经典名著也因你的阅读水平有限而远离你、抛弃你！残酷的现实已直逼每一个想学好英语又不知如何下手之人的心理防线！改变现状，势在必行！

　　为帮助同学们摆脱困扰，重树英语学习的信心，美国南加州大学英美文学专业研究学者，国内知名英语阅读推广人尹燕燕老师主编了这套"美国语文拓展阅读系列"丛书。该丛书选材丰富，贴近生活，内容涉及亲情、友情，感恩、信念，成长、改变，哲思、智慧等多个方面，包含各种激励人生前进的理念和生存智慧，而这些题材也是中小学作文中常常出现的话题。本书不仅为中英文写作提供了较好的范例和素材积累，而且可以让大家在充满快乐和温情的阅读中唤醒心灵，启迪人生。

　　书中的每篇文章除英中对照的主体内容外，还精选了世界名人的经典语录，简单的话语如春风拂面，耐人寻味；"词汇识记"和"短语搭配"两部分是大家积累词汇、熟识短语不可或缺的良师益友，而"译展身手"则为大家英语翻译应用以及日常交际提供了广阔平台。这些栏目的设置，可以帮助大家在阅读无障碍的同时，记单词、学语法、练翻译，彻底提高英语水平。

本书具有六大快速功效，适合所有想学好英语的人阅读学习。

第一，快速培养英语学习的乐趣，让你的英语学习不再枯燥；

第二，快速提高英语口语和阅读水平，让你的英语学习不再苦闷；

第三，快速识记词汇、巩固语法，让你的英语学习不再学了就忘；

第四，快速提升英语赏析能力，让你的英语学习不再乱无章法；

第五，快速提升英语翻译水平，让你见了老外不再畏首畏尾；

第六，快速提升英语综合能力，让你的英语水平全面升级！

如果你是一名正在学习英语的学生，阅读本书不仅可以提高英语阅读水平、中英文写作水平，还能让你开阔视野，陶冶情操，提高人文素养。

我国著名作家余秋雨曾说过："阅读的最大理由是想摆脱平庸，早一天就多一份人生的精彩；迟一天就多一天平庸的困扰。"现在，这本书就将带领大家重新审视自己的生活。相信它不仅可以帮你开拓视野，而且能触动你的心灵，让你早一天体会生活的精彩！

最后，祝大家开怀阅读，收获成功！

编者

目 录 CONTENTS

To Lead a Quiet Life
过一种淡泊宁静的生活

CONTENTS

Carrying "Regulators" in Their Hearts
随身携带心灵的"调节器"

The Export of Life
生命的出口

过一种淡泊宁静的生活

To Lead a Quiet Life

我们每天忙忙碌碌的，有时候，竟不知自己为什么而忙。

　　当生命想与你的心灵窃窃私语时，若你没有时间，你有两种选择：

　　倾听你心灵的声音或是让砖头来砸你!

不要在过道里徘徊吧，也别老惦记着你离车站还有多远!

　　为自己做点什么吧。

　　给自己留点时间，让你的身心都能好好休息下。

　　静静地坐着，听着抚慰心灵的轻音乐，或者从窗户看出去，欣赏大自然的奥妙奇景……

　　不论是什么让你觉得很特别很放松，去做就好。

　　生活得一边过一边瞧! 活在当下，享受当下，车站很快就会到达!

I Live Four Lives at a Time
我的四种生活

**Don't believe that winning is really everything. It's more important to
stand for something. If you don't stand for something, what do you win?**

—Lane Kirkland

I live a life of four dimensions—a wife, a mother, a worker, an
individual in society. Diversified roles, yes; but they are well knit by
two major forces: an attempt to discover, understand, and accept other
human beings; and a belief in my responsibility toward others. The first
began in my childhood when my father and I acted out Shakespeare.

He refused to let me merely parrot Hamlet's brooding soliloquy,
Lady Macbeth's sleepwalking scene, or Cardinal Woolsey's self-
analysis. He made a fascinating game of helping me understand the
motivations behind the poetic words.

In college, a professor further sparked this passionate curiosity
about the essence of others and, by his example, transmuted it into
a deep concern, a sense of responsibility that sprang not from stern
Calvinistic principles, but from an awareness of all I received—and
must repay with gladness.

I believe this acceptance, this tenderness one has for others, is impossible without an acceptance of self. Just when or where I learned that the full quota of human weakness and strength was the common property of each of us, I don't know. But somewhere in my late twenties, I grew able to admit my own drives—and, rid of the anguished necessity of recostuming them, I was free to face them, and recognize that they were neither unique nor uncontrollable.

The rich and happy life I lead every day brings new witness to the validity of my own philosophy, for me. Certainly it works in marriage. Any real marriage is a constant understanding and acceptance, coupled with mutual responsibility for one another's happiness. Each day I go out strengthened by the knowledge that I am loved and love.

In the mother-child relationship, those same two forces apply. Words are useless to describe my efforts to know my own children. But my great debt to them for their understanding of me is one I have often failed to repay. How can I overvalue a youngster with the thoughtfulness, the imagination to always phone when a late arrival might cause worry? To always know how to reassure. How can I repay the one who dashed into adulthood far too young but has carried all of its burden with a firm, joyous spirit?

My job itself is a reaffirmation of that by which I live. Very early in my working life, I was a small cog in a big firm. Emerging from a tiny job, I found a strange frightening world. Superficially, everyone was friendly. But beneath the surface were raging suspicion, distrust; the hand ever ready to ward off—or deliver—the knife in the back. For years I thought I was in a world of monstrous people. Then I began to know the company's president. I have no way of knowing what he had been. But at seventy, he was so suspicious, distrusting, that no one was telling him the truth. He had developed a technique of pitting all of us against each other. Able to see the distortion he caused, I youthfully declared that if I ran a business, it would be on the reverse principle.

For the last two years, I have had that opportunity, and had the joy of watching people—widely different people, too—learn to understand each other, accept each other, feel mutually responsible.

My trials and errors have really synthesized into one great belief, which is that I am not alone in my desire to reach my fellow man. I believe the human race is inherently cooperative and concerned about its brother.

不要认为取胜就是一切，更重要的是要有信念。倘若你没有信念，那胜利又有什么意义呢?

——莱恩·柯克兰

我在生活中有着四重身份——既为人妻，又为人母；既有自己的事业，又是社会的一分子。是的，角色不同，但配合得很好，因为它们都受两种主要力量的支配：一是努力观察、理解和接受他人，二是对他人尽职尽责。第一种努力早在孩童时代我和父亲一起"出演"莎剧时就开始了。

无论是哈姆雷特深沉的独白、麦克白夫人的梦呓，还是伍思里主教的自我剖析，父亲都不让我机械地背诵，而是通过有趣的游戏帮我揣摩诗句中隐含的角色内心活动。

　　在大学时代，一位教授的言传身教进一步引发了我理解他人本质的热忱与好奇，从他身上，我学到了如何将这种热忱与好奇转化为对他人深切的关爱、对他人应负的责任。这种责任心绝非源自卡尔文教派严格的教义，而是源自对我所获得一切的欣然回报。

　　我相信人若不能接受自己，便不可能接受和善待他人。不知从何时何地开始，我意识到每个人都有优点和缺点。在我快满三十岁的时候，我学会了承认内心的冲动，而非痛苦地将其掩饰，我泰然自若地应付它们，因为它们乃人之共性，只需善于驾驭。

　　我想我的人生哲学是正确的——我度过的充实而快乐的每一天便是明证。我的人生哲学也适用于婚姻生活，因为真正幸福的婚姻都建立在夫妻之间彼此不断理解和相互接受的基础之上，双方应尽职尽责，让对方幸福。每天我外出工作，知道我的爱得到了回报，便浑身有了力量。

　　这两种力量在母子关系之间也发挥了效用。我为了解孩子们所做出的努力远非文字所能形容，而孩子们对我的理解更让我无以为报。是怎样的想象力、心灵相通和体贴，让一个孩子在母亲迟迟未归时总是打电话确认她的行踪与安危？他用稚嫩的双肩快乐而坚定地担起成人的责任，我要怎样做才能报答这位早熟懂事的孩子?!

　　我的人生信条在工作中也得到了印证。从业之初，我只是一家大公司的无名小卒。我从低微的职位慢慢晋升，发现公司是个十分古怪而可怕的世界。每个人表面上和和气气，暗中却相互猜忌，人人自危，既怕自己背后射来暗箭，又想伺机捅人一刀。几年下来，我觉得公司里每个人都是魔鬼，后来才发现这一切都是总裁一手造成的。他从前为人如何我无从得知，但年已七旬的他满腹狐疑，不相信任何人，觉得所有人都在欺骗他，便运用手段挑起员工之间的争斗。明白了他何以能使人心扭曲，年轻的我暗下决心，他年我若自行创业，一定会运用完全相反的原则。

两年前我终于有机会自立门户，有了观察人的工作。我看到各种不同的人如何学会相互理解和接受，对彼此尽责。

我的尝试和成败得失熔铸成一个坚定的信念——绝非仅我一人试图理解与尊重他人。我相信合作与相互关爱正是人类的本性。

词汇识记

attempt [ə'tempt] *n.* 尝试，企图，努力
例：This was an attempt to close that chapter.
这也许是创造新开始的尝试。

professor [prə'fesə(r)] *n.* 教授，老师
例：My uncle is a professor in this university.
我的伯父是这所大学的一名教授。

overvalue ['əʊvə(r)'vælju:] *v.* 对……估价过高，过分重视
例：He should be careful not to overvalue himself.
他应该警惕自己不要自视过高。

declare [dɪˈklɛə(r)] v. 宣布，声明；宣称；申报

例：He declared that he was innocent.

他声称自己是无罪的。

opportunity [ˌɒpəˈtjuːnətɪ] n. 机会，时机

例：You must grasp this opportunity.

你必须抓住这次机会。

短语搭配

The first began in my childhood when my father and I acted out Shakespeare.

act out: 把……表演出来，把……付诸行动

造句：_____

How can I repay the one who dashed into adulthood far too young but has carried all of its burden with a firm, joyous spirit?

dash into: 冲进来

造句：_____

Emerging from a tiny job, I found a strange frightening world.

emerge from: 浮现，出现，（问题等）发生

造句：_____

译展身手

我相信，人如果无法接受自己，就不可能接受并善待他人。

译：_____

我看到各种不同的人如何学会相互理解和接受，对彼此尽责。

译：_____

Life as Chopsticks
人生如筷

A man is not old as long as he is seeking something. A man is not old until regrets take the place of dreams.

—John Barryomre

Chopsticks. Right now, millions of people are digging into their food with two sticks that have stood the test of time as a utensil for humans, even when countless thousands of other tools, gadgets and products haven't. But what's so special about them?

What can we learn from mere chopsticks?

Personally, I have used them all my life, but it was only recently that I realised the depth of influence they had in many people's way of life. They teach us the importance of:

Simplicity. They can come in all kinds of colours and sizes but essentially they are just two long sticks. There's hardly anything more simple than two bits of wood being pushed together. With new technology being released everyday and adverts bombarding us with the need to be able to do more with less, multi-tasking and multiple-use devices, it is sort of refreshing to still have something which has just one use—simply to eat. Chopsticks are a living example that simplicity simply works, and we don't need to keep developing, improving and fixing things all the time.

Versatility. Chopsticks can be used for picking up all kinds of food: meat, veg, rice, even the bones from fish, because by nature, their simplicity means that they are adaptable. Instead of aiming for a niche in an attempt to find a "gap in the market", or to fill a hole that probably doesn't need filling, they cater to a wide range purposes. Imagine being like chopsticks in this way, able to appeal to many people because you are useful, without worrying about being "more innovative"or "better" in anyway. They just do what they are made to do; they just are.

Aim. If you've ever tried using them, you know that you can't get what you want by just haphazardly stabbing at the plate. To be able to get what you want, you have to aim for it. There's no way you can pick up everything in one go. Know what you want, and just do it. Sometimes, a little bit of focus makes the difference between failure and success.

Practice. Using chopsticks doesn't come naturally. You have to learn to use them and practice it. But how will you learn? Should you just read about it? Most would agree that there's no better way to practice than to look at the delicious food in front of you and tell yourself that you can't have any until you can use the chopsticks to get it. In real life, you can read as much as you like about all the things you want to do, but it will just amount to dreams and theory if you don't try actually doing it. Don't just watch others eating, put yourself out there and give the chopsticks a go.

Slowing Down. A common health tip is to try to eat with chopsticks when you can. Why? Because it slows you down and allows your stomach to tell your brain you're full before you overeat. Eating with chopsticks is a slower process, but that is not necessarily a bad thing. Sometimes we need to slow down and take things one step at a time, break it down at each stage so that we have time to think, to realise that we're actually full and that we don't have to keep charging full speed through life.

Sometimes it's nice to enjoy each morsel of life as it comes.

只要一个人还有所追求，他就没有老。直到后悔取代了梦想，他才算老。

——约翰·巴里穆尔

筷子。现如今，当数不尽的工具、器具和产品都已被时间淘汰，只有筷子经受住了时间的考验，成千上万的人们用它们来夹取食物。那么它们到底有什么特别之处呢？

从这简简单单的筷子中，我们能学到什么？

对于我个人而言，我一生都在使用筷子，但直到最近，我才认识到它们深深地影响了许多人的生活方式。它们教会了我们许多重要的事：

简简单单。虽然筷子颜色各异，长短不同，但实质上，它们就是两根长棍。没有比两根靠在一起就能使用的木棍更简单的东西了。在科技日新月异的今天，铺天盖地的广告告诉我们应该使用那些事半功倍的多功能设备，筷子却仍旧保持着其单一的用途——就只是用来吃饭，这还真是与众不同啊。而筷子这个活生生的实例说明：简单的东西照样能派上大用场，我们并不需要一直改善更新，发展再发展。

运用广泛。筷子能用来夹取各种各样的食物，诸如肉、蔬菜、米饭等，还能用来挑鱼骨头，因为它们简单的本质意味着能屈能伸、适应性强。它们能满足各种广泛的要求，而非只瞄准于弥补某些市场缺口或者填补那些可能没必要填补的空白。想想筷子的哲学——用途广泛且不用担心被革新或被改善，所以深受人们喜爱。筷子只是做它本应做的，筷子就是筷子。

目标明确。如果你曾经试过用筷子吃饭，就会知道在餐盘上乱戳是夹不到你想要的东西的，必须得瞄准目标下筷。你不可能一下夹到所有东西，而应认清你要什么，然后努力得到它。成功或失败有时就在于那一点点的准确性。

熟能生巧。没人生来就会使用筷子。你必须要学着使用并不断练习。但是怎样学习呢？仅仅只是看使用说明吗？大部分人都同意最好的练习方法就是看着摆在眼前的美味食物，告诉自己不用筷子夹就不能吃。在现实生活中，你能（从书中）阅读到任何你想要做的事情，但是如果你不去试着实践，它们就仅仅只是梦想和理论。不要只看着别人吃，自己也去拿双筷子试试看。

放慢节奏。有一个众所周知的健康技巧是：尽可能使用筷子吃饭。为什么呢？因为它能让你放慢节奏，让肚子在吃撑前告诉大脑：你饱了。虽然用筷子吃饭是个较慢的过程，但这不见得是件坏事。有时我们需要放慢节奏，一步一步来，每个阶段停顿一下，以使我们有时间思考，认识到自己实际上已经饱了。我们没有必要总是保持高速冲刺的生活。

有时候，按部就班地享受生活的一点一滴是很幸福的。

词汇识记

realise ['rɪəlaɪz] *v.* 意识到；实现；明白

例：As I lay in that dark hour, I was aghast to realise that something was within me.

当我在黑夜里躺着的时候，我吃惊地体会到自己心里有某种东西。

technology [tek'nɒlədʒɪ] *n.* 技术，工艺

例：Anyone who tries to resist the spread of new technology is fighting a losing battle.

想阻止新技术传播的人注定要失败。

theory ['θɪərɪ] *n.* 学说，理论；原理；意见

例：Not everyone can understand Einstein's Theory of Relativity.

不是每个人都能读懂爱因斯坦的相对论的。

overeat [ˌəʊvər'iːt] *v.* 吃过量

例：Obese people find it difficult to stop overeating.

胖人觉得一吃就过量，难以控制。

短语搭配

Instead of aiming for a niche in an attempt to find a "gap in the market", or to fill a hole that probably doesn't need filling, they cater to a wide range purposes.

instead of: 代替，而不是

造句：＿＿＿＿＿＿＿＿＿＿＿＿＿＿＿＿＿＿＿＿＿

cater to: 满足……的需要；迎合

造句：＿＿＿＿＿＿＿＿＿＿＿＿＿＿＿＿＿＿＿＿＿

Sometimes we need to slow down and take things one step at a time…

slow down: 放慢（速度），（使）减速

造句：＿＿＿＿＿＿＿＿＿＿＿＿＿＿＿＿＿＿＿＿＿

译展身手

成功或失败有时就在于那一点点的准确性。

译：＿＿＿＿＿＿＿＿＿＿＿＿＿＿＿＿＿＿＿＿＿

有时候，按部就班地享受生活的一点一滴是很幸福的。

译：＿＿＿＿＿＿＿＿＿＿＿＿＿＿＿＿＿＿＿＿＿

Calmness of Mind
心灵的平静

We must accept finite disappointment, but we must never lose infinite hope.

　　　　　　　　　　　　　　　　　　—Mattin Luther King

　　Calmness of mind is one of the beautiful jewels of wisdom. It is the result of long and patient efforts in self-control. Its presence is an indication of ripened experience, and of a more than ordinary knowledge of the laws and operations of thought.

　　A man becomes calm in the measure that he understands himself as a thought evolved being, for such knowledge necessitates the understanding of others as the result of thought, and as he develops a right understanding, and sees more and more clearly the internal relations of things by the action of cause and effect he ceases to fuss and fume and worry and grieve, and remains poised, steadfast, serene.

　　The calm man, having learned how to govern himself, knows how to adapt himself to others; and they, in turn, reverence his spiritual strength, and feel that they can learn of him and rely upon him. The more tranquil a man becomes, the greater is his success, his influence, his power for good. Even the ordinary trader will find his business prosperity increase as he develops a greater self-control and equanimity, for people will always prefer to deal with a man whose demeanor is strongly equable.

The strong, calm man is always loved and revered. He is like a shade-giving tree in a thirsty land, or a sheltering rock in a storm. "Who does not love a tranquil heart, a sweet-tempered, balanced life?" It does not matter whether it rains or shines, or what changes come, for they are always sweet, serene, and calm. That exquisite poise of character, which we call serenity, is the last lesson of culture, the fruit-age of the soul. It is precious as wisdom, more to be desired than gold—yea, than even fine gold. How insignificant mere money seeking looks in comparison with a serene life—a life that dwells in the ocean of truth, beneath the waves, beyond the reach of tempests in the eternal calm!

"How many people we know who sour their lives, who ruin all that is sweet and beautiful by explosive tempers, who destroy their poise of character, and make bad blood! It is a question whether the great majority of people do not ruin their lives and damage the happiness by lack of self-control. How few people we meet in life who are well balanced, who have that exquisite poise which is characteristic of the finished character! "

Yes, humanity surges with uncontrolled passion, is tumultuous with ungoverned grief, is blown about by anxiety and doubt. Only the wise man, only he whose thoughts are controlled and purified, makes the winds and the storms of the soul obey him.

Tempest-tossed souls, wherever you may be, under what ever conditions you may live, know in the ocean of life the isle of blessedness are smiling, and the sunny shore of your ideal awaits your coming. Keep your hand firmly upon the helm of thought. Deep in your soul reclines the commanding master; he does but sleep; wake him. Self-control is strength; right thought is mastery; calmness is power. Say unto your heart, " Peace, be still!"

> 我们必须接受失望，因为它是有限的，但千万不可失去希望，因为它是无穷的。
>
> ——马丁·路德·金

心灵的平静是智慧的宝藏，它来自于长期、耐心的自我控制。内心的安宁是经历成熟的表现，也是对思想活动规律的更深入的了解。

一个人能否心境平和取决于他对自己的了解程度，因为如果他想了解别人，就必须先了解自己；当他对人对己有了更深入的了解，并越来越清晰地洞察到事物内部息息相关的因果关系时，他就不会再惊讶、愤怒、焦虑或悲伤，而是以从容、镇定、平和的态度去对待一切。

镇静的人知道怎样控制自己，也知道如何去适应与他人相处；反之，别人也会对他的人格魅力表示尊重，并会以他为榜样，认为他是个可靠的人。一个人越是处变不惊，他的成就、影响力和号召力就越大。即使是一个普通商人，如果他遇事能够很好地自我控制并镇定自若，那么他会发现自己的生意正在蒸蒸日上；因为人们总是更愿意与一个举止从容、沉着冷静的人打交道。

坚强、冷静的人总是会赢得人们的好感和敬意，他就像烈日下一棵浓荫遮地的大树，或是暴风雨中能够遮风挡雨的巨岩。"谁不爱一颗安静的心，一个温和、平实的生命呢？"无论是狂风暴雨，还是红日当空，无论是天翻地覆，还是命运逆转，一切都等闲视之，因为这样的人永远都是谦和、冷静、沉着的。那种我们称之为泰然自若的平静性格，是修养的最后一课，也是灵魂之花的硕果。它像智慧一样宝贵，价值胜过黄金——是的，胜过足赤真金。与宁静的生活相比，追逐名利的行为多么不值一提——那是一种在真理的海洋中的生活，在惊涛骇浪之下，远离暴风雨的侵扰，永远存在于宁静之中。

"我们认识的许多人都把自己的生活搞得一片狼藉，他们的怒火破坏了所有美好的事物，同时也摧毁了自己安静的生活，并遗祸后代！现在的问题是，大多数人是否因为缺乏自我控制能力而破坏了自己的生活，损毁了原有的幸福呢？在生活中，我们很少遇到能够做到沉着冷静、拥有成熟的性格所特有的那种平静的人。"

是的，人性因为无法控制的激情而躁动不安，因为放任无度的悲伤而起伏波动，因为焦虑和猜疑而备受打击。只有睿智的人，只有控制并净化了思想的人，才能在心灵的世界里呼风唤雨。

经历过暴风雨洗礼的人们，无论你们身在何方，无论你们处境如何，你们都要知道，在生活的海洋中，幸福的岛屿在对你微笑；照耀你理想的阳光就在前方。要牢牢握住思想之舵。在你的灵魂深处，有

一个指引你方向的主宰者，他可能还在沉睡，唤醒他吧。自我控制是力量，正确的思想是优势，沉着冷静是能量。要时常对你的心灵说："平和，安静！"

词汇识记

ordinary ['ɔ:dənrɪ] *adj.* 通常的，普通的；平庸的，平淡的

例：At first it looks quite ordinary, but there is nothing ordinary about it.

乍一看它很普通,其实它不普通。

calm [kɑ:m] *adj.* 平静的，冷静的

例：The calm sea gave no hint of the storm that was coming.

平静的海上没有一点迹象显示暴风雨即将来临。

adapt [ə'dæpt] *v.* 适应，适合

例：She adapted herself quickly to the new climate.

她很快就适应了这种新气候。

increase [ɪn'kri:s] *v.* 增加，提高

例：The company has increased the price of its cars.

公司已经提高了汽车价格。

precious ['preʃəs] *adj.* 珍贵的，贵重的

例：That old book is my most precious possession.

那本旧书是我最珍贵的财产。

Its presence is an indication of ripened experience, and of a more than ordinary knowledge of the laws and operations of thought.

more than: 超出……的

造句：_____

A man becomes calm in the measure... for such knowledge necessitates the understanding of others as the result of thought…

as the result of: 因为

造句：_____

心灵的平静是智慧的宝藏，它来自于长期、耐心的自我控制。

译：_____

他就像烈日下一棵浓荫遮地的大树，或是暴风雨中能够遮风挡雨的巨岩。

译：_____

在你的灵魂深处，有一个指引你方向的主宰者，他可能还在沉睡，唤醒他吧。

译：_____

Life Is Like a Cup of Coffee
生活就像杯中的咖啡

He who seizes the right moment, is the right man.

—Johann Wolfgang von Goethe

A group of graduates got together to visit their old university professor.

The conversation soon turned into complaints about stress in work and life. Offering his guests coffee, the professor went to the kitchen and returned with a large pot of coffee and a variety of cups—porcelain, plastic, glass, crystal, some plain-looking, some expensive, some exquisite—telling them to help themselves to the coffee.

When all the students had a cup of coffee in hand, the professor said, "If you have noticed, all the nice-looking expensive cups have been taken up, leaving behind the plain and cheap ones. While it is normal for you to want only the best for yourselves, that is the source of your problems and stress.

"Be assured that the cup itself adds no quality to the coffee. In most cases it is just more expensive and in some cases even hides what we drink.

"What all of you really want is coffee, not the cup, but you consciously went for the best cups... And then you began eyeing each other's cups.

"Now consider this: Life is the coffee; the jobs, money and position in society are the cups. They are just tools to hold and contain life, and the type of cup we have does not define, nor change the quality of life we live. Sometimes, by concentrating only on the cup, we fail to enjoy the coffee. Savor the coffee, not the cups! Don't let the cups drive you... enjoy the coffee instead."

谁把握机遇，谁就心想事成。

——约翰·沃尔夫冈·歌德

一群毕业生，各自在事业上都已有所建树，相约一起去看望他们年老的大学教授。

谈话一会儿就变成了各自对工作和生活压力的抱怨。在用咖啡招待这些客人时，教授去厨房端来一大壶咖啡，并拿出各式各样的咖啡杯——陶瓷的、塑料的、玻璃的、水晶的，有看上去普通的、有价值不菲的、有做工精细的——让他们自己倒咖啡喝。

当所有学生手中都端了一杯咖啡后，教授发话了："如果你们注意一下，就会发现所有好看的昂贵的杯子都被挑走了，剩下的只

是那些普通的和便宜的。当然，每个人都只想拥有最好的，这很正常，但这也是你们的问题和压力的根源所在。

"可以肯定的是，杯子本身与咖啡质量毫无关系。在很多时候，杯子让咖啡更昂贵，某些时候，甚至让我们看不清我们要喝的是什么。

"其实你们真正想要的是咖啡，而不是杯子，但你们却又都下意识地去挑选最好的杯子，并观察别人拿到的杯子。

"现在设想一下：如果生活是杯中的咖啡，工作、财富和社会地位就是那些杯子。他们只是维持生活的工具而已，并不改变生活质量。有时候，我们在过于关注杯子的同时却忘记了去品味上帝赐予的咖啡。所以，不要成为杯子的奴隶……好好品味杯中的咖啡。"

词汇识记

conversation [ˌkɒnvəˈseɪʃn] *n.* 谈话，会话

例：He told the newspapermen about the conversation, but would not play them the actual tape of it.

他向新闻记者讲了这次谈话的情况，却不愿把实况录音磁带放给他们听。

variety [vəˈraɪətɪ] *n.* 多样，种类，多样化
例：The hotel offers its guests a wide variety of amusements.
这个旅馆为住客提供了各种各样的娱乐活动。

assure [əˈʃɔː(r)] *v.* 使确信，使放心，确保
例：I can assure you that your son will be happy here.
我可以向你保证，你儿子在这里会很快乐的。

短语搭配

A group of graduates got together to visit their old university professor.
get together: 聚会，聚集；达成一致
造句：＿＿＿＿＿＿＿＿＿＿＿＿＿＿＿＿＿＿＿＿＿＿
The conversation soon turned into complaints about stress in work and life.
turn into: 变成
造句：＿＿＿＿＿＿＿＿＿＿＿＿＿＿＿＿＿＿＿＿＿＿

译展身手

如果你们注意一下，就会发现所有好看的昂贵的杯子都被挑走了，剩下
的只是那些普通的和便宜的。
译：＿＿＿＿＿＿＿＿＿＿＿＿＿＿＿＿＿＿＿＿＿＿
可以肯定的是，杯子本身与咖啡质量毫无关系。
译：＿＿＿＿＿＿＿＿＿＿＿＿＿＿＿＿＿＿＿＿＿＿
其实你们真正想要的是咖啡，而不是杯子。
译：＿＿＿＿＿＿＿＿＿＿＿＿＿＿＿＿＿＿＿＿＿＿

Two Ways of Life
人生的两条路

Victory won't come to me unless I go to it.

—M. Moore

It was New Year's night. An aged man was standing at a window. He raised his mournful eyes towards the deep blue sky, where the stars were floating like white lilies on the surface of a clear calm lake. When he cast them on the earth, where few more hopeless people than himself now moved towards their certain goal—the tomb. He had already passed sixty of the stages leading to it, and he had brought from his journey nothing but errors and remorse. Now his health was poor, his mind vacant, his heart sorrowful, and his old age short of comforts.

The days of his youth appeared like dreams before him, and he recalled the serious moment when his father placed him at the entrance of the two roads—one leading to a peaceful, sunny place, covered with flowers, fruits and resounding with soft, sweet songs; the other leading to a deep, dark cave, which was endless, where poison flowed instead of water and where devils and poisonous snakes hissed and crawled.

He looked towards the sky and cried painfully, "Oh, youth, return! Oh, my father, place me once more at the entrance to life, and I'll choose the better way!"But both his father and the days of his youth had passed away.

He saw the lights flowing away in the darkness. These were the days of his wasted life; he saw a star fall from the sky and disappeared, and this was the symbol of himself. His remorse, which was like a sharp sorrow, struck deeply into his heart. Then he remembered his friends in his childhood, which entered life together with him. But they had made their way to success and were now honored and happy on this New Year's night.

The clock in the high church tower struck and the sound made him remember his parents' early love for him. They had taught him and prayed to God for his good. But he chose the wrong way. With shame and grief he dared no longer to look towards the heaven where his father lived. His darkened eyes were full of tears, and with a despairing effort, he burst out a cry: "Come back, my early days! Come back!"

And his youth did return, for all this was only a dream, which he had on New Year's night. He was still young though his faults were real; he had not yet entered the deep, dark cave, and he was still free to walk on the road which leads to the peaceful and sunny land.

Those who still linger on the entrance of life, hesitating to choose the bright road, remember that when years are passed and

your feet stumble on the dark mountains, you will cry bitterly, but in vain. "Oh youth, return! Oh give me back my early days!"

胜利是不会向我们走来的，我必须自己走向胜利。

——穆尔

　　这是新年的夜晚。一位老人站在窗边，忧伤的眼睛眺望着深蓝的天空。空中的繁星犹如漂浮在清澈如镜的湖面上的朵朵百合。他慢慢将目光投向地面，此刻，没有什么人比他还绝望，因为他即将迈向他最终的归宿——坟墓。他已走过通向坟墓的六十级台阶，除了错误和悔恨，他一无所获。现在，他体弱多病，精神空虚，心哀神伤，人到晚年无慰藉。

　　年轻岁月，如梦般展现在他面前，老人想起父亲把他带到岔路口的那个庄严时刻——一条路通向安宁、快乐的世界，鲜花遍布，果实丰硕，甜美轻柔的歌声在空中回荡；另一条路则通向幽深黑暗，没有尽头的洞穴，洞内流淌着的不是水而是毒液，群魔乱舞，毒蛇嘶嘶爬动。

　　他仰望星空，痛苦地大喊："啊，青春，回来吧！啊，父亲，再一次带我到人生的岔路口吧，我会选一条更好的道路。"但是，他的父亲和青春岁月都已经一去不复返了。

他看到亮色在黑暗中流逝，就像他挥霍掉的往昔；他看到一颗流星自天边坠落，消失不见，就像是他的化身。无尽的悔恨，像一支利箭，深刺心间。他又记起和自己一同迈入人生之途的儿时玩伴。但他们已功成名就，在这个新年之夜，备受尊崇，幸福快乐。

高高的教堂钟楼传来敲钟声，这声音使他记起父母早年对他的疼爱。他们教育他，为他祈祷。然而，他却选择了错误的道路。羞愧和悲哀使他再也没有勇气仰望父亲所在的天堂。黯淡的双眼噙满了泪水，他绝望地嘶声大呼："回来吧，我的往昔! 回来吧!"

他的青春真的回来了，所有这些只是一个梦，一个他在新年之夜所做的梦。他仍然年轻，虽然他犯的错误是真实的；他尚未走入那幽深黑暗的洞穴，还有自由选择通向安宁、快乐的道路。

仍在人生路口徘徊，仍在为是否应当选择光明坦途而犹豫不决的人们啊，请记住：当青春不再，当你的双脚在黑暗的山岭间跌绊时，你会痛苦地呼喊："啊，青春，回来吧! 啊，还给我往昔吧!"此时，一切已是徒劳。

词汇识记

recall [rɪˈkɔːl] *v.* 召回，恢复，回想起，唤起；与……相似
例: The danger recalled him to a sense of duty.
这危险的事唤起了他的责任感。

peaceful ['pi:sfəl] *adj.* 和平的，安宁的

例：We hope there will be a peaceful transition to the new system.

我们希望能够和平过渡到新的制度。

disappear [ˌdɪsə'pɪə(r)] *v.* 不见，消失

例：The sun disappeared behind a cloud.

太阳消失在一片云后面。

pray [preɪ] *v.* 祈祷，祈求；请求，恳求

例：I pray God's forgiveness.

我祈求上帝的宽恕。

短语搭配

His darkened eyes were full of tears, he burst out a cry: "Come back, my early days! Come back!"

burst out: 大声喊叫，突然……起来

造句：_____

Those who still linger on the entrance of life... but in vain.

in vain: 徒然，白费力

造句：_____

译展身手

一位老人站在窗边，忧伤的眼睛眺望着深蓝的天空。

译：_____

他看到亮色在黑暗中流逝，就像他挥霍掉的往昔。

译：_____

What's Happiness
什么是幸福

Most folks are about as happy as they make up their minds to be .

—Abraham Lincoln

"Are you happy?" I asked my brother, Ian, one day. "Yes. No. It depends on what you mean, " he said. "Then tell me, " I said, "when was the last time you think you were happy?" "April 1967, " he said.

It served me right for putting a serious question to someone who has joked his way through life. But Ian's answer reminded me that when we think about happiness, we usually think of something extraordinary, a pinnacle of sheer delight. And those pinnacles seem to get rarer the older we get.

For a child, happiness has a magical quality. I remember making hide-outs in newly cut hay, playing cops and robbers in the woods, getting a speaking part in the school play. Of course, kids also experience lows, but their delight at such peaks of pleasure as winning a race or getting a new bike is unreserved.

In the teenage years, the concept of happiness changes. Suddenly it's conditional on such things as excitement, love, and popularity. I can still feel the agony of not being invited to a party that almost everyone else was going to.

In adulthood the things that bring profound joy — birth, love, marriage — also bring responsibility and the risk of loss. Love may not last, loved ones die. For adults, happiness is complicated.

My dictionary defines happy as "lucky" or "fortunate", but I think a better definition of happiness is "the capacity for enjoyment". The more we can enjoy what we have, the happier we are. It's easy to overlook the pleasure we get from loving and being loved, the company of friends, the freedom to live where we please, even good health.

I added up my little moments of pleasure yesterday. I spent an uninterrupted morning writing, which I love. When the kids came home, I enjoyed their noise after the quiet of the day.

You never know where happiness will turn up next. When I asked friends what makes them happy, some mentioned seemingly insignificant moments. A friend loves the telephone. "Every time it rings, I know someone is thinking about me."

We all experience moments like these. Too few of us register them as happiness.

While happiness may be more complex for us, the solution is the same as ever. Happiness isn't about what happens to us; it's about how we perceive what happens to us. It's the knack of finding a positive for every negative, and viewing a setback as a challenge. It's not wishing for what we don't have, but enjoying what we do possess.

对于大多数人来说，他们认定自己有多幸福，就有多幸福。

——亚伯拉罕·林肯

"你幸福吗？"一天我问我的兄弟伊恩。"又幸福，又不幸福。这要看你指的是什么，"他说。"那么告诉我，"我说，"你最近一次感到幸福是什么时候？""1967年4月。"他说。

向一个游戏人生的人提问这么严肃的问题，我真是自讨苦吃。但是伊恩的话启发了我，当我们考虑幸福的时候，我们通常想到一些不同寻常的事情和愉快无比的时刻。而随着年龄的增长，这种时刻似乎越来越少。

对于孩子来说，幸福充满了魔力。我记得在新割下的草堆里捉迷藏，在树林里扮演警察和强盗，在校剧中担当有台词的角色。当然孩子也有情绪低落的时候，但是当赢了赛跑或得到一辆新自行车时，他们流露出的快乐是无可比拟、没有任何保留的。

到了少年时期，幸福观发生了变化。突然间幸福有了条件，例如：刺激、爱情和名气等。我还能感受到因未被邀请去参加一个几乎人人有份的晚会所体会到的痛苦。

　　成年时，能带来深深欢乐的事情——如出生、爱情和婚姻，同时也带来了责任和失去的危险。爱情也许难以持久，心爱的人也许会离开人世。对于成年人来说，幸福是复杂的。

　　我的字典把幸福定义为"幸运"或"好运"，但是我想幸福更好的定义是"享受的能力"。我们越能享受所拥有的一切，我们就越幸福。从爱与被爱、友情、随心所欲择地而居，甚至到拥有的健康，其中获得的快乐很容易被我们忽视了。

　　我总结了一下我昨天的幸福时刻。过了一个写作不受干扰的上午，令我愉快；等到孩子们回家，我享受安静的一天过后他们吵闹的声音。

　　你永远无法知道下一次幸福何时来临。我问朋友们什么能使他们感到幸福，一些人举出一些似乎不太重要的时刻。一位朋友喜欢接电话，"每次电话铃声响，我就知道有人正想着我呢。"

　　我们都经历过类似的事，但视之为幸福的人却寥寥无几。

　　虽然幸福对我们来说也许更错综复杂，但是获得幸福的途径永远是一样的。幸福不在于我们的遭遇如何，而在于我们如何看待所遭遇到的事情。这是化消极为积极、将挫折看作挑战的诀窍。幸福不是凭空许愿，而是享受拥有。

词汇识记

experience [ɪkˈspɪərɪəns] v. 经历，体验，感受

例：We learn from the past, experience the present and hope for success in the future.

我们从过去中学习，体验现在，展望未来的成功。

profound [prəˈfaʊnd] *adj.* 深奥的，极度的，意义深远的
例：We all have profound admiration and respect for him.
我们都非常钦佩和尊敬他。

responsibility [rɪˌspɒnsəˈbɪlətɪ] *n.* 责任，职责，责任心
例：Our teacher has a high sense of responsibility.
我们老师有高度的责任感。

solution [səˈluːʃn] *n.* 解决办法，解答
例：We haven't found the solution yet, but I'm sure we're on the right track.
我们还没有找到解决办法，但我肯定我们的思路是对的。

短语搭配

It depends on what you mean ...

depend on: 依靠；依赖

造：_____

I added up my little moments of pleasure yesterday.

add up: 合计

造：_____

译展身手

对于成年人来说，幸福是复杂的。

译：_____

幸福不是凭空许愿，而是享受拥有。

译：_____

Say Goodbye to Yourself
跟自己说拜拜

I am a slow walker, but I never walk backwards.

—Abraham Lincoln

One day not too long ago the employees of a large company in St. Louis, Missouri, returned from their lunch break and were greeted with a sign on the front door. The sign said, "Yesterday the person who has been hindering your growth in this company passed away. We invite you to join the funeral in the room that has been prepared in the gym."

At first everyone was sad to hear that one of their colleagues had died, but after a while they started getting curious about who this person might be.

The excitement grew as the employees arrived at the gym to pay their last respects. Everyone wondered: "Who is this person who was hindering my progress? Well, at least he's no longer here!"

One by one the employees got closer to the coffin, and when they looked inside it they suddenly became speechless. They stood over the coffin, shocked and in silence, as if someone had touched the deepest part of their soul.

There was a mirror inside the coffin: everyone who looked inside it could see himself. There was also a sign next to the mirror that said, "There is only one person who is capable of setting limits on your growth: it is YOU."

You are the only person who can revolutionize your life. You are the only person who can influence your happiness, your realization and your success. You are the only person who can help yourself.

Your life does not change when your boss changes, when your friends change, when your parents change, when your partner changes, or when your company changes. Your life changes when YOU change, when you go beyond your limiting beliefs, when you realize that you are the only one responsible for your life.

我走得很慢，但是我从来不会后退。

——亚伯拉罕·林肯

不久前的某天，密苏里州圣路易斯一家大公司的职员外出吃完午饭，刚踏进前门，一则讣告迎面而来："公司里面老是妨碍你进步的人昨天去世了。我们邀请您到体育馆专设的灵堂参加葬礼。"

起初，每一个人都为失去一位同事而难过，可不一会儿，大伙都不禁开始好奇起来：这个人会是谁呢？

　　随着抵达体育馆向遗体告别时刻的到来，大家感到越来越兴奋，"我的绊脚石到底是谁？"这个问题萦绕在每个人的心头，"幸好他已经去世了！"

　　大伙紧跟着依次走近灵柩。当他们往里面看的时候，突然变得异常安静。他们站在灵柩旁，沉默、震惊，就像有人拨动了他们灵魂最深处的某根神经。

　　那里面躺着的是一面镜子！大伙看到的人就是自己。镜子旁边还写着文字："能牵绊你的人只有一个——你自己！"

　　你是唯一能让你改头换面的人。你是唯一能让你欢喜让你忧，让你成功让你失败的人。唯一能帮助你的人，就是你自己！

　　老板、公司变了，朋友、父母、伴侣变了，你的生活不会因此而改变。可一旦你改变了，你超越了自己，有了自我负责的意识，你的生活就会发生改变。

词汇识记

growth [grəʊθ] *n.* 增长，生长，发展，种植

例：We are entering a period of rapid population growth.

我们正在进入人类快速增长的时期。

prepare [prɪˈpɛə(r)] *v.* 预备，准备

例：He is preparing his speech for the meeting tomorrow.

他正准备明天集会的演说。

silence ['saɪləns] *n.* 沉默，寂静

例：There was nothing but silence in the room.

这间屋内声息全无，一片寂静。

influence ['ɪnfluəns] *v.* 影响，感染

例：Don't let me influence your decision.

不要让我影响你的决定。

短语搭配

At first everyone ... but after a while they started getting curious about...

after a while: 过一会儿，不久

造句：_____

Well, at least he's no longer here!

at least: 至少

造句：_____

There is only one person who is capable of setting limits on your growth...

be capable of: 有能力，能够，可以

造句：_____

译展身手

公司里面老是妨碍你进步的人昨天去世了。

译：_____

唯一能帮助你的人，就是你自己！

译：_____

Dealing with Worry
学会"放下"

No wind serves him who addresses his voyage to no certain port.

—Michel de Montaigne

A professor began his class by holding up a glass with some water in it. He held it up for the students to see and asked them, "How much do you think this glass weighs?"

"1 pound!" "2 pounds!" "3 pounds!"... the students answered.

"I really don't know unless I weigh it, " said the professor, "but, my question is: What would happen if I held it up like this for a few minutes?"

"Nothing, " the students said.

"OK. What would happen if I held it up like this for an hour?" the professor asked.

"Your arm would begin to ache, " said one of the students.

"You're right. Now what would happen if I held it for a day?"

"Your arm could go numb. You might have severe muscle stress and paralysis and you would have to go to the hospital for sure, " ventured another student. All the students laughed.

"Very good. But during all this, did the weight of the glass change?"

asked the professor.

"No, " replied the students.

"Then what caused my arm to ache? The muscle stress? What should I do?"

The students were puzzled.

"Put the glass down, " said one of the students.

"Exactly!" said the professor. "Life's problems are something like this. If you hold them for a few minutes in your head, you seem OK. But if you think of them for a long time, you begin to ache. Hold them even longer and then they begin to paralyze you. You will not be able to do anything. It is important to think of the challenges in your life. It is even more important to 'put them down' at the end of every day before you go to sleep. This way, you will not be overwhelmed, and will wake up every day fresh, strong and capable of handling any issue or any challenge that comes your way!"

Remember friend.—put the glass down today!

航行若没有确定的目的港，风绝不会助他一臂之力。

——米歇尔·德·蒙田

教授举起一个装着水的玻璃杯，开始了他的讲课。他高举杯子好让所有的学生都能看到，然后问道："你们觉得这个玻璃杯有多重？"

学生纷纷回答道："1磅！""2磅！""3磅！"……

教授说道："不称的话我也不知道。但是，我要问的问题是：如果我就这样举着，几分钟后，会发生什么事情？"

学生答道："什么都不会发生。"

教授继续问道："好。那我要是这样举一个小时呢？"

一个学生说道："您的手臂会疼。"

"没错，现在，我要是这样举一天，会怎么样？"

另一个学生小心地说道："那您的手臂会发麻。您可能会因为承受严重的肌肉压力而感觉到麻痹。您肯定要上医院。"所有的学生都笑了。

"非常好。但是，在上述情况发生的时候，杯子的重量改变了吗？"教授问道。

学生回答："没有。"

"那么，是什么引起了手臂疼痛？肌肉压力吗？我该怎么办？"

学生都迷惑了。

其中一个学生回答道："（您可以）把杯子放下。"

教授说道："没错！生活中的问题和这类似。如果你在脑海里想它们几分钟，没什么问题。但是如果你长时间想着它们，你会开始感觉疼痛。想的时间更长点，它们就会让你麻痹，你什么也做不了。对生活中的挑战进行反思，这很重要。但是更重要的是，你要在每天上床睡觉前把它们'放下'。这样，你就不会觉得难以承受，就能每天醒来充满活力，得心应手地处理那些妨碍你前进的问题或挑战！"

朋友，记住，今天就把"杯子"放下！

词汇识记

weigh [weɪ] *v.* 称（重量），重达……

例：A full-grown elephant can weigh over 6,000 kilograms.

一头成年大象能重达六千多公斤。

unless [ən'les] *conj.* 除非，如果不

例：I won't go to the party unless I'm invited.

除非我被邀请，否则我不会去参加晚会的。

stress [stres] *n.* 压力，强调

例：I can't bear the stresses of modern life.

我不能忍受现代生活的压力。

puzzled [pʌzld] *adj.* 困惑的，迷惑的

例：She listened with a puzzled expression on her face.

她脸上带着困惑的表情在倾听。

短语搭配

A professor began his class by holding up a glass with some water in it.

hold up: 举起，阻挡，耽搁

造句：_____

It is even more important to 'put them down' at the end of every day ...

at the end of: 在……末端，到……尽头

造句：_____

This way, you will not be overwhelmed, and will wake up every day fresh ...

wake up: 醒来，叫醒

造句：_____

译展身手

如果我就这样举着，几分钟后，会发生什么事情？

译：_____

对生活中的挑战进行反思，这很重要。

译：_____

Home
家

In this world there is always danger for those who are afraid of it.

—George Bernard Shaw

What is home? A roof to keep out the rain? Four walls to keep out the wind? Floors to keep out the cold? Yes, but home is more than that. It is the laugh of a baby, the song of a mother, the strength of a father, warmth of loving hearts, lights from happy eyes, kindness, loyalty, and comradeship.

Home is the first school for young ones, where they learn what is right, what is good and what is kind; where they go for comfort when they are hurt or sick; where joy is shared and sorrow eased; where fathers and mothers are respected and loved, and children are wanted; where the simplest food is good enough for kings because it is earned; where money is not as important as love and kindness; where even the tea kettle sings from happiness. That is home.

There is a magical place in our own private universe that stays at the core of our being no matter where our life's journeys take us. It is where we seek refuge when the slings and arrows of outrageous fortune have become too much for the soul to bear.

Home beckons the child in us who cries out above the din of conflicting sounds and clashing egos. It is like an unseen hand that lulls us to blissful slumber, a strong shoulder upon which we can cast our never-ending burdens, and an invisible light that warms the innermost of our hearts. It lets us forget our fears for the time being, bringing us back to more transcendent time when we were children.

Ah, the time when we were children. Wasn't it the most pristine period of our existence? It is the time of our life when laughter was easy, dreams were for free, moments were tender, and troubles were a world away.

And home, sweet home, was the safest place to be. Inside its walls we were protected from the pains of growing up, taking them all in, and letting them go. Its air allowed us to breathe generously the fresh smell of morning sunshine, animals in pasture, flowers in bloom and soft breeze blowing from the horizon.

It is a virtual reservoir of the loveliest thoughts and fondest memories of our life. Mostly we spent to be wished for again and again a harbor where things and faces are warm and familiar, giving and nurturing, caring and everlasting.

It is where we shed our superficial selves, repair our tired bodies, boost our depressed spirits, fix our tarnished psyches, mend our bruised emotions and change our evil ways.

When we were in the simplicity of our youth, all that we had were dreams to spin, rainbows to chase, stars to wish upon, and dewdrops to catch. Home shapes the persons we are today. It stirs passions long laid dormant, letting it all break out and fall free. And we always emerge the better for allowing ourselves to delight in the breathtaking review of pathways and old, familiar places; the welcoming embrace of cherished faces; and the fond memories not at all faded by time.

Indeed, more often than not, we stray too far to places unknown in search of what we need, what we want and what we would die for just to have —and we return home to find it.

对于害怕危险的人，这个世界上总是危险的。

——乔治·萧伯纳

家是什么？避雨的屋檐，遮风的四壁，还是御寒的地板？是的，这些都是家的一部分，但是这还远远构不成家。家里还要有婴儿的笑声、妈妈的歌声、爸爸的力量、爱的温暖、幸福的眼神、善意、忠诚和同志之谊。

家是孩子们的第一所学校，在那儿他们知道了什么是对，什么是好，什么是善。当他们受到伤害或是生病时，会从那里得到温暖和安慰。在那里，欢乐得到分享，忧伤得到缓解；在那里，爸爸、妈妈互相尊重，孩子们被需要；在那里，最简单的食物也美味得足以飨国王，因为那是自己赚来的；在那里，钱没有爱心和善意重要；在那里，就是茶壶也在唱着幸福的歌谣。那就是家。

　　在我们的心中有一个神奇的地方，不管生命之旅把我们带到何处，它都是我们生命的核心。当恶境中的枪林弹雨让我们的身心感到难以承受时，我们会在那里寻求到庇护。

　　在世事的喧嚣和自我的冲突中，家召唤着我们心中的童真。它就似一只看不见的手轻抚着我们安然进入甜美的梦乡；也似那强壮的臂膀，可以承载起我们无尽的负担；还似一盏看不见的明灯，温暖着我们的内心深处。它让我们忘掉了现时的恐惧，超越时空带我们回到了童年。

　　啊，童年，那不是我们一生最质朴、最纯洁、最崇高的时候吗？那时候，我们自在地笑，自由地梦想，一幕幕总是那么温柔，烦恼与麻烦离我们是那么遥远。

　　家，甜蜜的家，那是我们最安全的地方。在它的保护下，我们免受了成长所带来的痛苦，它容纳了我们所有的伤痛，又化解了它们。它的空气使我们可以畅快地呼吸早晨阳光下的清新气息，牧场上动物的气息，盛开的花朵那令人神清气爽的香气，还有那从地平面吹拂而来的清凉微风。

　　它实际上是一个蓄水池，储存着我们最可爱的想法和最美妙的回忆。其实我们生命大部分的努力都是为了得到一个港湾，在那里所有的物品和脸庞都是温暖而又熟悉的，准备给予而又滋润人的，充满关爱而又永恒的。

　　在这里，我们可以脱掉虚饰的外衣，休养疲惫的身体，重振萎靡的精神，拭亮黯淡的心灵，养护我们受伤的情感，改正我们心中的邪恶。

　　在我们单纯的青年时代，我们现在所拥有的一切都还是梦，是待追逐的彩虹，待摘下的星星，待采撷的露珠。是家造就了我们今天的自己。是家激起了我们潜伏已久的热情，使其爆发、释放。当我们快乐地回望常走的路、熟悉的老地方、珍爱的人对你欢迎的拥抱以及没有随着时间流逝而褪色的美好回忆时，那总是让我们很感动，我们的精神面貌也总是会随之焕然一新。

确实，我们为了寻求我们需要和渴望的东西，为了寻求我们而愿意献出自己生命而拥有的东西，我们常常到那些全然陌生的地方，迷失在那里——只有当我们回到家中，才发现原来我们要找的就在家里。

词汇识记

comfort ['kʌmfət] *n.* 舒适，安逸，安慰，慰藉
例：They are now living in relative comfort.
他们现在过着比较安逸的生活。

burden ['bə:dn] *n.* 负担，责任
例：The burden on his back seemed to be crushing him to the earth.
他背上的重负似乎要把他压倒在地。

existence [ɪgˈzɪstəns] *n.* 存在，生存
例：According to some philosopher, everything in existence is reasonable.
某位哲学家认为，存在的事物都是合理的。

passion ['pæʃn] *n.* 激情，热情，酷爱

例：He has a passion for photography.

他对摄影有强烈的爱好。

indeed [ɪn'diːd] *adv.* 真正地，的确，事实上

例：I was very glad indeed to hear the news.

听到这消息我的确非常高兴。

短语搭配

Inside its walls we were protected from the pains of growing up...

protect from: 保护……不受损害，使……免受损害

造句：_____

It stirs passions long laid dormant, letting it all break out and fall free.

break out:（战争、火灾等）爆发，逃脱

造句：_____

Indeed, more often than not, we stray too far to places unknown in search of what we need...

in search of: 寻找，寻求

造句：_____

译展身手

家，甜蜜的家，那是我们最安全的地方。

译：_____

是家造就了我们今天的自己。

译：_____

在平常的生活中寻找不平常
Seek for Unusual

当你给自己设定了一个目标之后，你是踌躇满志还是心存怀疑？

　　当你没有如愿实现自己的目标时，你是不是就此降低对自己的期望？

在你的人生历程中，如果有人给予你帮助或传授你智慧，你要心怀感激地接受。

永远相信：无论你做什么，你终究会成功，并且不要忘记坚持、自律和决心的价值。

当想象力放飞了你的才能时，你就能实现任何目标。

你注定会成为你梦想要成为的那个人。

A Lesson About Courage
自由奔跑

Ordinary people merely think how they shall spend their time; a man of talent
tries to use it.

—Arthur Schopenhauer

One afternoon, many years ago, I went to pick up my mother from
work. I got there a little early so I parked the car by the road, across the
street from where she worked, and waited for her.

As I looked outside the car window to my right, there was a small
park where I saw a little boy, around one and a half to two years old,
running freely on the grass as his mother watched from a short distance.
The boy had a big smile on his face as if he had just been set free
from some sort of prison. The boy would then fall to the grass, get up,
and without hesitation or without looking back at his mother. Run as
fast as he could, again, still with a smile on his face, as if nothing had
happened.

However, with kids (especially at an early age), when they fall
down, they don't perceive their falling down as failure, but instead, they
treat it as a learning experience (as just another result outcome). They
feel compelled to try and try again until they succeed. (The answer must

be... they have not associated "falling down" with the word "failure" yet, thus they don't know how to feel the state accompanies failure. As a result, they are not disempowered in anyway. Plus, they probably think to themselves that it's perfectly okay to fall down, that it's not wrong to do so. In other words, they give themselves permission to make mistakes, subconsciously. Thus they remain empowered.)

While I was touched by the boy's persistence, I was equally touched by the manner in which he ran. With each attempt, he looked so confident... so natural. No signs of fear, nervousness, or of being discouraged—as if he didn't care about the world around him.

His only aim was to run freely and to do it as effectively as he could. He was just being a child—just being himself completely in the moment. He was not looking for approval or was not worried about whether someone was watching or not. He wasn't concerned about being judged. He didn't seem to be bothered by the fact that maybe

someone would see him fall (as there were others in the park aside from him and his mother) and that it would be embarrassing if he did fall. No, all that mattered to him was to accomplish the task or activity at hand to the best of his ability. To run ... and to feel the experience of running fully and freely. I learned a lot from that observation and experience, and have successfully brought that lesson with me in my many pursuits in life.

Since then, I've always believed that in each of us is a little child with absolute courage. A child that has the ability to run freely (or express himself fully and freely)—without a care for anything external—without a care for what people would say if he/she experiences a fall. I believe that that courageous part of us, that courageous child within us all, will always be with us for as long as we live. We only need to allow it to emerge more fully. We only need to once again connect with that child within us—and give that child permission to run freely, just like that boy in the park.

普通人只想到如何度过时间，有才能的人设法利用时间。

——亚瑟·叔本华

多年前，有一天下午，我去接妈妈下班。到了那儿后，时间还有些早。于是，我把车子停在路边，在她工作单位的街对面等着。

我从右侧的车窗往外望去，看见一个小公园里有一个小男孩，大约一岁半到两岁之间。他正在草地上自由奔跑，他的妈妈在附近注视着他。小男孩笑得非常灿烂，好像刚从某种监禁中释放出来一样。偶尔，他在草地上摔倒了，但又毫不犹豫地爬起来继续跑，也不回头看他的妈妈，就像什么也没发生过似的，仍面带微笑地继续以最快的速度奔跑。

然而，对于小孩子来说(尤其是幼童)，当他们摔倒在地，并不认为那是失败。相反，他们会像对待学习经验一样(或者只是另一种结果甚至成就)，不断地去尝试，直到成功。（原因一定是他们并不把"摔倒"与"失败"联系起来，他们并不知道如何去感受这种情形伴随而来的失败。所以，无论如何，他们都不会有挫败感。另外，他们可能认为自己摔倒也没什么，这样并没有什么错。换言之，在他们的潜意识里，容许自己犯错。这样，他们总是充满活力。）

小男孩的坚持打动了我，他奔跑的方式也同样令我深深地感动。他的每一次尝试，看起来都那么自信，那么自如，没有一丝恐惧、紧张或气馁——好像对他周围的世界毫不在意。

自由奔跑是他唯一的目

标，他只是尽全力地去跑。他只是一个孩子——在那个时刻，完完全全地表现他真正的自我。他没有寻求称赞，也不担心是否有人在看着他，更不在乎他人的评判。他看上去并不为自己摔倒可能会被别人看到而感到难堪(因为在公园里，他和妈妈旁边还有其他人)。他全心全意地去完成任务，或者说尽最大的能力完成手头上的活动，去奔跑……全身心地去感受自由自在的奔跑。从那次观察及其感受中，我得到了很多启示，并把这些启示成功地运用到我的许多人生追求当中。

　　从那以后，我总是相信，我们每一个人都有一颗绝对勇敢的童心。一个孩子能全心投入地自由奔跑(或毫不掩饰地表现真我)——对外在环境毫不在意——即使摔倒，对别人的言论也毫不在意。我相信，我们都有这样的勇气，都有这样一颗勇敢的童心，这种勇敢会伴随我们一生。我们只要全身心投入地表露出来，只要再次连接这颗童心——让孩子般的宽大放任身心自由奔跑，就像公园里的那个小男孩一样。

词汇识记

associate [əˈsəʊʃieit] *v.* 联想，联系；（使）联合；结交

例：She associated happiness with having money.

她把幸福和有钱联想到一起。

confident [ˈkɒnfɪdənt] *adj.* 有信心的，自信的；确信的，肯定的

例：Your encouragement made me more confident of my future.

你的鼓励使我对我的未来更加有信心。

concerned [kən'sə:nd] *adj.* 担忧的，关心的，关切的，有关的

例：Concerned parents held a meeting.

忧心忡忡的家长们开了一次会。

courageous [kə'reɪdʒəs] *adj.* 勇敢的

例：He is such a courageous man that he does not fear death at all.

他是一个非常勇敢的人，所以一点也不怕死。

短语搭配

One afternoon, many years ago, I went to pick up my mother from work.

pick up: 拿起；取，接；学会；好转；继续

造句：_____

The boy had a big smile on his face as if he had just been set free from some sort of prison.

as if: 好像，仿佛

造句：_____

The boy would then fall to the grass, get up, and without hesitation or without looking back at his mother.

without hesitation: 毫不踌躇地

造句：_____

译展身手

他看上去并不为自己摔倒可能会被别人看到而感到难堪。

译：_____

从那以后，我总是相信，我们每一个人都有一颗绝对勇敢的童心。

译：_____

A Glass of Milk
一杯奶可以温暖我们一辈子

One thing I know: The only ones among you who will be really happy are those who will have sought and found how to serve.

—A. Schweizer

One day, a poor boy who was trying to pay his way through school by selling goods door to door found that he only had one dime left. He was hungry so he decided to beg for a meal at the next house.

However, he lost his nerve when a lovely young woman opened the door. Instead of a meal he asked for a drink of water. She thought he looked hungry so she brought him a large glass of milk. He drank it slowly, and then asked, "How much do I owe you."

"You don't owe me anything, " she replied. "Mother has taught me never to accept pay for a kindness. " He said, "Then I thank you from the bottom of my heart. " As Howard Kelly left that house, he not only felt stronger physically, but it also increased his faith in God and the human race. He was about to give up and quit before this point.

Years later the young woman became critically ill. The local doctors were baffled. They finally sent her to the big city, where specialists can be called in to study her rare disease. Dr. Howard Kelly, now famous was called in for the consultation. When he heard the name of the town she came from, a strange light filled his eyes. Immediately, he rose and went down through the hospital hall into her room.

Dressed in his doctor's gown he went in to see her. He recognized her at once. He went back to the consultation room and determined to do his best to save her life. From that day on, he gave special attention to her case.

After a long struggle, the battle was won. Dr. Kelly requested the business office to pass the final bill to him for approval. He looked at it and then wrote something on the side. The bill was sent to her room. She was afraid to open it because she was positive that it would take the rest of her life to pay it off. Finally she looked, and the note on the side of the bill caught her attention. She read these words...

"Paid in full with a glass of milk. "

(Signed) Dr. Howard Kelly

Tears of joy flooded her eyes as she prayed silently: "Thank You, God. Your love has spread through human hearts and hands."

有一点我是知道的：在你们之中，只有那些愿意寻求发现如何为别人服务的人，才是真正幸福的。

——施韦泽

一天，一个贫穷的小男孩为了攒够学费正挨家挨户地推销商品。饥寒交迫的他摸遍全身，却只有一角钱。于是他决定向下一户人家讨口饭吃。

然而，当一位美丽的年轻女子打开房门的时候，这个小男孩却有点不知所措了。他没有要饭，只乞求给他一口水喝。这位女子看到他饥饿的样子，就倒了一大杯牛奶给他。男孩慢慢地喝完牛奶，问道："我应该付多少钱？"

年轻女子微笑着回答："一分钱也不用付。我妈妈教导我，施以爱心，不图回报。"男孩说："那么，就请接受我由衷的感谢吧！"说完，霍华德·凯利就离开了这户人家。此时的他不仅自己浑身是劲儿，而且更加相信上帝和整个人类。本来，他都打算放弃了。

数年之后，那位女子得了一种罕见的重病，当地医生对此束手无策。最后，她被转到大城市医治，由专家会诊治疗。大名鼎鼎的霍华德·凯利医生也参加了医疗方案的制订。当他听到病人来自的那个城镇的名字时，一个奇怪的念头霎时间闪过他的脑际。他马上起身直奔她的病房。

身穿手术服的凯利医生来到病房，一眼就认出了恩人。回到会诊室后，他决心一定要竭尽所能来治好她的病。从那天起，他就特别关照这个对自己有恩的病人。

经过艰苦的努力，手术成功了。凯利医生要求把医药费通知单送到他那里，他看了一下，便在通知单的旁边签了字。当医药费通知单送到她的病房时，她不敢看。因为她确信，治病的费用将会需要她花费整个余生来偿还。最后，她还是鼓起勇气，翻开了医药费通知单，旁边的那行小字引起了她的注意，她不禁轻声读了出来：

"医药费已付：一杯牛奶。"

（签名）霍华德·凯利医生

喜悦的泪水溢出了她的眼睛，她默默地祈祷着："谢谢你，上帝，你的爱已通过人类的心灵和双手传播了。"

词汇识记

physically ['fɪzɪkli] *adv.* 身体上

例：After his vacation he was in fine condition both physically and mentally.

度假之后，他的身体状况和精神状况都很好。

consultation [ˌkɒnsl'teɪʃn] *n.* 商量；会诊

例：The doctors held a consultation to decide whether an operation was necessary.

医生们进行会诊，决定是否需要动手术。

request [rɪ'kwest] *v.* 请求，要求

例：He was requested to report back to the committee about/on the complaint.

委员会要求他对投诉事件做出调查报告。

approval [ə'pruːvl] *n.* 赞成，同意；批准，认可

例：She smiled her approval.

她以微笑表示同意。

短语搭配

One day, a poor boy who was trying to pay his way through school by selling goods door to door found that he only had one dime left.

door to door: 挨家挨户，送货上门的

造句：_____

From that day on, he gave special attention to her case.

from that day on: 从那天起

造句：_____

译展身手

我妈妈教导我，施以爱心，不图回报。

译：_____

你的爱已通过人类的心灵和双手传播了。

译：_____

The Important Words to Change Your Life
改变你生活的重要话语

A man can fail many times, but he isn't a failure until he begins to blame somebody else.

—J. Burroughs

The most important messages that humans deliver to one another often come in just three words. Think of "I love you" or "There's no charge" or "And in conclusion".

One of the phrases that I've found most useful is this: "I'll be there."

I'll be there. If you've ever had to call a plumber over a weekend, you know how good these words can feel. If you've heard them after being stranded on the road with car trouble and used your last quarter to call a friend, you've known the feeling too.

"Grandma, I'm graduating in June!" I'll be there.

"Mom, the baby cries all night, and if I don't get some sleep I'll perish!" I'll be there.

One person who really knows how to "be there" is Elizabeth, the Queen Mother of England. During the Blitz on London in 1940, she was asked whether the little princesses, Elizabeth and Margaret Rose, would leave England for their safety. The queen replied:

"The children will not leave unless I do. I shall not leave unless their father does, and the king will not leave the country in any circumstances whatever. "

I'll be there.

Another important three-word phrase is one of the hardest to learn to say—I know it was for me. It is: Maybe you're right.

If more people would say "maybe you're right," the marriage counselors would go out of business. I know from experience it can have a disarming effect in an argument. When we're so hung up on getting our own way that we won't concede on any point, we do ourselves a real disservice.

I must have heard the next phrase a thousand times when I was a little person and faced a hard decision. Turning to my nanny, I'd ask what I should do. Her response was always the same: Your heart knows.

"My heart knows?" I would grumble. "What's that supposed to mean? I need advice here. I need you to tell me what to do. "

She would just smile and say, "Your heart knows, honey. Your heart knows."

But I was an imperious child. I would throw my hand on my hip and say. "Maybe so, but my heart isn't talking!"

To this she would respond, "Learn to listen."

People may suggest what we should do, but for the most part no one will accept responsibility for our mistakes. We have to make our own choices. That's when we need to listen. Your heart knows.

Psychologists call this "tuning in to ourselves". Spiritual leaders call it, "turning to a higher power". Whatever you call it, you have the ability to find the right answers for your life. It's a powerful gift but you have to learn to use it.

It took me a long time. but I learned that life doesn't come with a plan. To some extent the page is blank. You may have a rough outline of where you are going, but you won't get there without making some tough decisions. To this end, you may find these simple, yet profound, words helpful.

一个人可以失败很多次，但是只要他没有开始责怪旁人，他还不是一个失败者。

——巴勒斯

人们往往只需三个字就能彼此传递最重要的信息。想想那些"我爱你""免费"，还有"综上所述"。

但我发现最有用的一句是"我就来"。

我就来。如果你周末曾经打电话向管道工求助，你就知道这句话有多受用；如果你因车子抛锚在路上而束手无策，你用最后一分钱拨通了朋友的电话，你就会明白这种感觉了。

"奶奶，我六月份就要毕业了！"我准去。

"妈妈，宝宝整晚哭个不停，我再不休息会儿会崩溃的！"我就来。

真正懂得如何做到"就来"的是当时的英国女王伊丽莎白。1940年伦敦受闪电战袭击时，有人问她两位小公主伊丽莎白与玛格丽特·罗丝会不会为了安全起见而离开英格兰。女王这么答道：

"我不走，孩子们不会走；她们的父亲不走，我绝不会走；而她们的父亲是无论如何都不会扔下国家不管的。"

我会坚守阵地。

另外一个重要的"六字经"是最难以启齿的——我过去就是如此。那就是：也许你是对的。

如果更多的人说上这句"也许你是对的"，婚姻咨询顾问恐怕就要失业。依我的经验，这句话能让一场争论"灰飞烟灭"。当我们固执己见、寸步不让时，我们其实就是搬起石头砸自己的脚。

小时候面临抉择时，下面的"五字经"我听过无数遍。那时我总是问奶妈怎么做，而她的回答始终如一：你心里明白。

"我心里明白？"我嘟囔着。这是什么鬼意思？"我要的是建议，我要你告诉我该做什么。"

她只是笑笑说："你心里明白，宝贝。"

但我太专横，会双手叉腰："也许是，但我的心不会说话！"

到这时她才会说："那就学着聆听。"

别人可以建议我们该做什么，但在大多数情况下，没有人会为我们的错误承担责任，我们得自己做决定。那就是我们聆听的时候。你心里明白！

心理学者称之为"倾听心声"，宗教领袖称之为"求助于神的力量"。不管你把它叫什么，你都有能力为自己的人生找到正确的答案。此句具有强大威力——但你得学会如何运用才行。

我花了很长时间才明白，生活是无法事先规划的，从某种程度上说，生活是一片空白。对于你生活的方向，你能制定一个大致的框架，但要达到目标，却要做出艰难的选择。至此，你可能明白了这些简单但深邃的话语是多么有益。

词汇识记

deliver [dɪ'lɪvə(r)] *v.* 交付，解救
例：They prayed to God to deliver them from danger.
他们祈求上帝把他们从危险中拯救出来。

graduate ['grædʒʊət] *v.* 毕业
例：Mary was graduated from Oxford.
玛丽毕业于牛津大学。

respond [rɪ'spɒnd] *v.* 回答，答复；(to)做出反应，响应
例：I invited her to dinner but she did not respond.

我请她吃晚饭，但她未做回答。

blank [blæŋk] *adj.* 空白的；茫然的

例：I can't think of where I've left my umbrella; my mind's a complete blank!

我想不起来把伞丢在哪儿了，一点印象都没有！

短语搭配

Think of "I love you" or "There's no charge" or "And in conclusion".

in conclusion: 最后，总之

造句：_____

The king will not leave the country in any circumstances whatever.

in any circumstances: 不管情况如何

造句：_____

If more people would say "maybe you're right," the marriage counselors would go out of business.

go out of business: 歇业

造句：_____

译展身手

小时候面临抉择时，下面的"五字经"我听过无数遍。

译：_____

我不走，孩子们不会走。

译：_____

至此，你可能明白了这些简单但深邃的话语是多么有益。

译：_____

A Lesson Is Repeated Until Learned
走出重复

We always have time enough, if we will but use it aright.

—Johann Wolfgang von Goethe

Have you ever noticed that a lesson tends to repeat themselves? Does it seem as if you married or dated the same person several times in different bodies with different names? Have you run into the same type of boss over and over again? If you don't deal well with authority figures at home, then you will have an opportunity to deal with them out in the world. You will continually draw into your life people who need to enforce authority, and you will struggle with them until you learn the lesson of obedience.

You will continually attract the same lesson into your life. You will also draw to your teachers to teach you that lesson until you get it right. You may try to avoid the situation, but they will eventually catch up with you. The only way you can free yourself of difficult patterns and issues you tend to repeat is by shifting your perspective so that you can recognize the patterns and learn the lessons that they offer. To face these challenges means you need to accept the fact that something within you keeps drawing you to the same kind of person or issue, though that situation or relationship may be very painful.

The challenge, therefore, is to identify and release the patterns that you are repeating. This is no easy task, since it means you have to change, and change is not always easy. Staying just as you are may not help you advance spiritually, but it certainly is comfortable in its familiarity.

Rising to the challenge of identifying and releasing your patterns forces you to admit that the way you have been doing things isn't working. The good news is that by identifying and releasing the pattern, you actually learn how to change. In order to facilitate your process of change, you will need to learn the lessons of willingness and patience.

Once you master these, you will most likely find the challenge of identifying and releasing your patterns far less intimidating.

The real secret to being able to change is the willingness to do so. If you are to make any progress in excavating yourself from the cycles that entrap you, you must first identify the patterns that keep you stuck. Then you can begin to release the old behaviors.

If you truly want to change, you will choose to do it, and make a commitment to the process of it. However, if you rely on the thought that you should change, you will make the decision to do so and then you will feel the pinch of sacrifice. Following the current

trends, the advice of friends, or the wishes of family members result in decision; following your inner compass results in choice.

So when you are struggling to make a change in your life, ask yourself, "How willing am I, really, to make this change?" If you are not succeeding, there's a good chance that you may be relying on your belief that you should change, rather than on your intrinsic desire to do so.

Patience is the display of tolerance while awaiting an outcome. You are presented with the lesson of patience the moment you try to create a change within yourself. You expect immediate results and are often disappointed when your first few attempts to follow through fall short. When people who try to lose weight cheat on their diets, they get very frustrated with themselves for not being able to stay with their new eating regime and berate themselves for not changing their patterns.

As you already know, change is rarely easy, and you need to exercise gentleness and patience with yourself as you work your way through this process. Growth can be a slow, painstaking process and patience will provide you with the stamina you need to become the person you want to be.

If you absolutely hate getting stuck in traffic, chances are that you need a little work in the area of patience. And, chances are, you will probably get stuck in more traffic that someone who has no issue with patience—and not simply because the universe has a sense of humor. You will just notice the traffic more than someone who has more patience.

Remember, a lesson will be repeated until learned. It just takes a little patience.

只要我们能善用时间，就永远不愁时间不够用。

——约翰·沃尔夫冈·歌德

　　你是否曾注意到，生活中的教训总是重复出现。这看起来是不是就像与你结婚或多次约会的始终是同一个人，只不过是身材和名字不同罢了呢？你是否曾多次遇到相似类型的老板呢？如果你无法同家中的掌权者处理好关系，那么，你在外面的世界同样会遇到这种状况。你的生活会不断地陷入强权者的控制中，而且，你会一直与之对抗，直到学会服从为止。

　　在你的生活中，会不断地出现相同的教训。你会吸引老师前来教你，直到你完全明白为止。你可能会努力避免这种情形，但终究会身陷其中。唯一能让你从这些重复不断的艰难模式和问题中解脱出来的方法是：转变你的观念，这样你就能认清这些模式，并从中吸取教训。直面这些挑战意味着你要接受一个事实：你自身的某些因素使你的生活重复出现同类型的人或问题，尽管你可能会为这种情形或关系倍感痛苦。

　　所以，这个挑战就是要辨明你不断重复的行为模式，并从中解脱。这是一个艰巨的任务，因为，它意味着你必须做出改变，而改变往往不容易，但停滞不前不利于你心灵的成长，虽然它确实让你有舒适的熟悉感。

面对这个挑战，要辨明自己的行为模式并从中解脱，那么，你必须承认，你过去曾有过某种行不通的行为方式。可喜的是，通过辨明这种模式并解脱出来，你会真正学会如何去改变。为了协助你改变的进程，你会学会积极和忍耐。一旦掌握了这些，你很可能会发现辨明这种模式并从中解脱并不是特别艰难。

改变的真正秘诀是你愿意这样去做。如果你在挣脱困住你的模式的过程中取得了任何进展，那你首先应该辨明被困的模式，然后开始摆脱以前的习惯。

如果你真正想改变，就要选择去做，并真正付诸行动。但是，如果你只是觉得自己应该改变，就要下定决心。然后，你会感受到牺牲的痛苦。跟随当今的潮流，听从朋友的建议，或迫于家人的期望，都会促使你做出决定，而你应该在心灵罗盘的指引下来选择。

所以，当你努力想改变生活时，先扪心自问，"我想做出这个改变的决心到底有多大？"如果你没有答案，那么，你很可能认为自己应该改变，但在你的内心深处并没有这种渴望。

耐心是在等待结果时显示出来的承受力。一旦你准备改变

自我，就要耐心面对。你期望立刻有结果，并往往会为开始的几次尝试没有成功而失望。当人们试着减肥，却无法抗拒美食时，便会对自己不能执行新的饮食计划而倍感失望，并为不能改变生活模式而自责不已。

正如你所知，改变通常很艰难。当你处于改变的过程中时，要对自己宽容，并耐心地去练习。成长是一个缓慢而艰苦的过程，耐心会让你更有毅力，帮助你去做自己想做的人。

如果你对堵车深恶痛绝，那么你应该多培养自己的耐心。另外，你可能会比那些有耐心的人更频繁地遭遇堵车——不是因为上天捉弄你，而是与那些有耐心的人比起来，你对堵车更在意。

记住，一个教训总会反复出现，直到你学会为止。它只不过更需要耐心而已。

词汇识记

avoid [ə'vɔɪd] v. 避免，避开

例：If we are to avoid defeat we need a change of leadership.

我们要避免失败的话，就要换掉领导人。

spiritually ['spɪrɪʃuəli] *adv.* 精神上

例：I felt spiritually very depressed.

我精神上感到很压抑。

challenge ['tʃælɪndʒ] *n.* 挑战；质问

例：This career offers a challenge.

这份职业具有挑战性。

outcome ['aʊtkʌm] *n.* 结果，后果

例：The outcome of the election is a foregone conclusion.

选举结果已在预料之中。

短语搭配

You may try to avoid the situation，but they will eventually catch up with you.

catch up with: 赶上；对……产生恶果

造句：＿＿＿＿＿＿＿＿＿＿＿＿＿＿＿＿＿＿＿

When people who try to lose weight cheat on their diets, they…

lose weight: 减肥

造句：＿＿＿＿＿＿＿＿＿＿＿＿＿＿＿＿＿＿＿

译展身手

如果你真正想改变，就要选择去做，并真正付诸行动。

译：＿＿＿＿＿＿＿＿＿＿＿＿＿＿＿＿＿＿＿

记住，一个教训总会反复出现，直到你学会为止。

译：＿＿＿＿＿＿＿＿＿＿＿＿＿＿＿＿＿＿＿

The Differences Between Friendship and Love
友情和爱情的区别

Love is the joy of the good, the wonder of the wise, the amazement of the gods; desired by those who have no part in him, and precious to those who have the better part in him.

—Plato

Both are so much related to each other. And both are so dissimilar! What are the differences between friendship and love? Is platonic friendship possible between persons of opposite sex? Let us try and understand.

What is friendship? Why do we call a person our friend? When do we call someone a very good friend? If we care for a person, if we are always ready to help that person and if we share most of our thoughts with a person, they are our good friends. We can always count upon our good friends in an emergency. We are always sure that our friend will understand why we acted in a certain way. We need not explain anything to our very good friends. The friendship is so deep and the relationship is so intimate, that most of the things are automatically understood by our friends.

What about love? In a relationship of deep love, all the sharing that we discussed above are taken for granted. But love transcends all this. During love, we are attached with a particular person, while in friendship, one may have many friends. A loving relationship makes one so much attached to the other, that one gets pained if his / her beloved is hurt! Love also involves a physical element. Friendship does not have that. This is a vital difference. Nature gives us love so that the species can go forward. Nature does not give us friendship.

Your heart beats will never increase in anticipation of meeting your friend. You will not lie awake at night thinking about your friend. You will not feel totally lost, if you don't meet your friend for a few days. You will not have dreams in your eyes thinking about your friend. But in love, you will do all this and much more. Indeed, there is no comparison between love and friendship.

爱是美好带来的欢欣，智慧创造的奇观，神仙赋予的惊奇。缺乏爱的人渴望得到它，拥有爱的人又万般珍惜它。

——柏拉图

　　两者联系是如此密切，两者却又那么截然不同。友情和爱情有什么区别？异性朋友间的理想化的友谊真的存在吗？我们来试着分析一下。

　　什么是友情？为什么我们管一个人叫"朋友"？什么时候我们管一个人叫作"好朋友"？如果我们关心一个人，我们总是准备帮助那个人，如果我们和某个人分享大部分的想法，那个人一定是我们的好朋友。在紧急情况下我们总是依靠好朋友。我们总是确定好友会理解我们行事的方式。我们不需要向亲密的朋友解释什么。友情如此深，关系如此牢，以至于朋友间的事双方都会很自然地理解。

　　什么是爱情？在深爱中，上面我们讨论的事情都是理所当然的。但是爱情远远超过这些。恋爱中，我们总是和某个人关系密切。但是在友情中，一个人可能有很多朋友。恋爱的两个人联系得如此紧密，如果他/她受到了伤害，另一个人也会心痛。爱情总会有身体上的接触。友情却没有。这是至关重要的区别。上苍给予了我们爱情，以使

种族延续。但是上苍却没有给我们友情。

在盼朋友出现时，你的心跳不会加快；你不会夜不能寐地想着你的朋友；如果几天没见到朋友，你也不会完全迷失；想到朋友时，你的眼中不会有梦想。但是在恋爱中，这一切你都会做而且程度会更深。确实，爱情和友情没有可比性。

词汇识记

share [ʃeə(r)] *v.* 分享，分担

例：If you want a share of the pay, you'll have to do your fair share of the work.

要是你想得到一份报酬，你就必须做好你该分担的那一份工作。

relationship [rɪˈleɪʃənˌʃɪp] *n.* 关系，关联

例：There is a relationship between diet and cancer.

饮食结构和癌症之间有一定关联。

attach [əˈtætʃ] *v.* 连接

例：We are much attached to each other.

我们之间感情深厚。

species [ˈspiːʃiːz] *n.* 种类，（单复同）物种

例：We should do our best to save endangered species.

我们应该竭尽全力挽救濒于灭绝的生物。

短语搭配

Both are so much related to each other.

be related to: 与……相关

造句：_____

If we care for a person, if we are always ready to help…

care for: 照顾，喜欢

造句：_____

You will not lie awake at night thinking about your friend.

think about: 考虑

造句：_____

译展身手

如果我们和某个人分享大部分的想法，那个人一定是我们的好朋友。

译：_____

友情如此深，关系如此牢，以至于朋友间的事双方都会很自然地理解。

译：_____

但是在友情中，一个人可能有很多朋友。

译：_____

Making the Tacks
做鞋钉

Try not to become a man of success but rather try to become a man of value.

—Albert Einstein

The hardworking blacksmith Jones used to work all day in his shop and so hard working was he that at times he would make the sparks fly from his hammer.

The son of Mr. Smith, a rich neighbor, used to come to see the blacksmith every day and for hours and hours he would enjoy himself watching how the tradesman worked.

"Young man, why don't you try your hand to learn to make shoe tacks, even if it is only to pass the time?" said the blacksmith. "Who knows, one day, it may be of use to you."

The lazy boy began to see what he could do. But after a little practice he found that he was becoming very skilled and soon he was making some of the finest tacks.

Old Mr. Smith died and the son on account of the war lost all his goods. He had to leave home and was forced to take up residence in another country. It so happened that in this village there were numerous shoemakers who were spending a lot of money to buy tacks for their shoes and even at times when they paid high prices they were not always able to get what they wanted, because in that part of the country there was a high demand for soldiers' shoes.

Our young Mr. Smith, who was finding it difficult to earn his daily bread, remembered that once upon a time he had learned the art of making tacks and had the sudden idea of making a bargain with the shoemakers. He told them that he would make the tacks if they would help to get him settled in his workshop. The shoemakers were only too glad of the offer. And after a while, Mr. Smith found that he was soon making the finest tacks in the village.

"How funny it seems," he used to say, "even making tacks can bring a fortune. My trade is more useful to me compared to all my former riches."

不要为成功而努力，要为做一个有价值的人而努力。

——阿尔伯特·爱因斯坦

琼斯是个非常勤劳的铁匠，常常一整天都在店里工作。他工作非常努力，他的铁锤下常常是火花飞舞。

邻居史密斯先生很有钱，他的儿子常常来看琼斯打铁。他喜欢看这位工匠工作，常常一看就是几个小时。

"年轻人，为什么不亲自尝试一下如何制作鞋钉呢，哪怕只是为了消磨时间？"铁匠说，"没准，有一天它会对你有帮助。"

懒懒的孩子开始想看看自己到底能做什么。然而，仅仅经过很短的练习，他便发现自己非常熟练起来，很快他就做出了最好的鞋钉。

老史密斯先生去世了，而他的儿子则因为战争的缘故失去了所有的财产。他不得不离开家园，在另外一个国家住了下来。巧的是，这个国家的这个地区，急需大量军鞋，所以这个村子里有很多鞋匠，他们总是花费很多钱购买鞋钉。有时，即使付了很高的价钱，也买不到他们想要的鞋钉。

在这食不果腹的困难时刻，年轻的史密斯记起自己曾学过制鞋钉这门手艺，便突发奇想，想和这些鞋匠们做一个交易。他对他们说，如果他们可以帮助他成立一个店铺，他就可以做鞋钉。鞋匠们对他的这一提议欣喜若狂。很快，史密斯发现他做的鞋钉是村里面最好的。

"这真是有趣，"他常常会说，"即便是做鞋钉也会带来财富。与我以前所有的财富相比，我现在做的事情对于我来说更有用。"

词汇识记

blacksmith [ˈblæksmɪθ] *n.* 铁匠，锻工

例：Joe had to work as blacksmith in place of his lazy father.

乔只得代替他懒惰的父亲去当铁匠。

residence ['rezɪdəns] *n*. 居住

例：I want to insure my residence.

我要为自己的住宅保险。

bargain ['bɑ:gɪn] *n*. 交易

例：The leaders bargained away the freedom of their people.

领导人拿人民的自由来做交易。

短语搭配

Old Mr. Smith died and the son on account of the war lost all his goods.

on account of: 因为，由于

造句：_____

He had to leave home and was forced to take up residence in another

country.

take up: 开始从事；把……继续下去；着手处理；占去

造句：_____

The shoemakers were only too glad of the offer.

be glad of: 因……而高兴

造句：_____

译展身手

他工作非常努力，他的铁锤下常常是火花飞舞。

译：_____

与我以前所有的财富相比，我现在做的事情对于我来说更有用。

译：_____

What Do You Focus on
发现生活真精彩

Life can only be understood backwards, but it must be lived forwards.

—Kierkegaard

At Washington D. C. Metro Station on a cold January morning, a man played six Bach pieces for about an hour. During that time, approximately two thousand people went through the station, most of whom were on their way to work.

After 3 minutes, a middle-aged man noticed that there was a musician playing. He slowed his pace, stopped for a few seconds and then hurried to meet his schedule.

4 minutes: the violinist received his first dollar. A woman threw the money in the box and, without stopping, continued to walk.

6 minutes: a young man leaned against the wall to listen to the violinist, then looked at his watch and started to walk again.

10 minutes: a 3-year-old boy stopped but his mother tugged him along hurriedly as the kid looked at the violinist. Finally the mother pushed hard and the child continued to walk, turning his head all the time.

Several other children repeated this action. Every parent, without exception, forced them to move on.

45 minutes: the musician continued to play. Only 6 people stopped and stayed for a while. About 20 gave him money but continued to walk at their normal pace.

He collected $32.

After a hour, the musician finished playing and silence took over. No one noticed, no one applauded, nor was there any recognition.

No one knew this but the violinist was Joshua Bell, one of the best musicians in the world. He played one of the most intricate pieces ever written, with a violin worth $3.5 million dollars two days before he sold out a theater in Boston where the seats averaged $100.

This is a real story. Joshua Bell's playing incognito at the metro station was organized by the *Washington Post* as part of a social experiment about perception, taste and priorities of people.

The questions rose: In a commonplace environment, at an inappropriate hour, do we perceive beauty? Do we stop to appreciate it? Do we recognize talent in an unexpected context?

If we do not have a moment to stop and listen to one of the best musicians in the world, playing some of the finest music ever written, with one of the most beautiful instruments, how many other things are we missing?

只有向后才能理解生活；但要生活好，则必须向前看。

——克尔凯郭尔

　　某个寒冷的一月早晨，在华盛顿哥伦比亚特区地铁站，一个男人花了约一个小时，演奏了六支巴赫的曲子。在这期间，有大约两千人经过，其中大部分为上班族。

　　演奏开始3分钟后，一个中年男人注意到了一个音乐人正在演奏。他放慢了脚步，甚至停下来了几秒钟，然后为了赶时间，匆忙离去。

　　4分钟后，这位小提琴手收到了第一个一美元。那是一个妇女扔到盒子里的，她甚至没有停下来，就继续往前走。

　　6分钟后，一个年轻的男人斜靠着墙在那儿听小提琴手演奏，然后看了一下手表后，就开始继续他的旅程。

　　10分钟后，一个三岁的男孩停了下来，但是被他的妈妈匆匆忙忙拽走了，小孩边走还边看小提琴手。最后，小孩的妈妈只好使劲推着他走，小孩只好继续前进，但还一直回头看。

　　另外有几个小孩也做出了相同的举动。而每位家长无一例外地强迫他们继续往前走。

45分钟后，音乐人继续演奏。只有六个人停下来，并停留了一小会儿。约20个人给了他钱但是并没有减慢他们的正常步速。

他总共收到了32美元。

一个小时后，音乐人结束了演奏，车站恢复了原来的安静。没有人注意到，没有人鼓掌，更没有人认出他来。

没有人知道这位小提琴手就是世界上最好的音乐家之一——约舒亚·贝尔。他用一把价值350万美元的小提琴演奏了史上最复杂的曲子之一。两天后，约舒亚·贝尔在波士顿一家剧院的音乐会门票被抢购一空，平均每张售价100美元。

这是一个真实的故事，约舒亚·贝尔隐姓埋名在地铁站演出是《华盛顿邮报》专门安排的，是一个为了调查人们的感觉、品味和喜好而进行的社会实验中的一部分内容。

问题是，在最平凡不过的环境中，在一个不合时宜的时间段里面，我们感知到美了吗？我们有停下来欣赏美了吗？我们在意想不到的情况下认出天才了吗？

如果我们连停下来聆听由一位世界上最好的音乐家用一件最美丽的乐器演奏的一些最好的曲子的时间都没有，那

么，对于其他的东西，我们又错失了多少？

词汇识记

schedule [ˈʃedjuːl] *n.* 时间表，一览表，计划
例：Owing to various delays, we arrived two days behind schedule.
由于种种耽搁，我们比原计划迟到了两天。

lean [liːn] *v.* 倾斜，依靠，倚
例：He leans on the back of the sofa.
他斜靠在沙发的背上。

collect [kəˈlekt] *v.* 收集，聚集
例：We are collecting money for the famine victim.
我们在为遭受饥荒的灾民募捐。

taste [teɪst] *n.* 味觉，味道，品味，爱好
例：She has good taste in clothes.
她对服装有很好的审美眼光。

短语搭配

During that time, approximately two thousand people went through the station ...
go through: 经历，检查，浏览
造句：_____
Every parent, without exception, forced them to move on.

without exception: 毫无例外地

造句: _____

He played ... before he sold out a theater in Boston where the seats averaged $100.

sell out: 卖完，背叛，出卖

造句: _____

译展身手

演奏开始3分钟后，一个中年男人注意到了一个音乐人正在演奏。

译: _____

一个小时后，音乐人结束了演奏，车站恢复了原来的安静。

译: _____

What Do You Hear
你听到了什么

Some people are moulded by their admirations, others by their hostilities.

—Elizabeth Bowen

A Native American and his friend were in downtown New York City, walking near Times Square in Manhattan. It was during the noon lunch hour and the streets were filled with people.

Cars were honking their horns, taxis were squealing around corners, and the sounds of the city were almost deafening. Suddenly, the Native American said, "I hear a cricket."

His friend said, "What? You must be crazy. You couldn't possibly hear a cricket in all of this noise!"

"No, I'm sure of it," the Native American said, "I heard a cricket."

"That's crazy," said the friend.

The Native American listened carefully for a moment, and then walked across the street to a big planter where some shrubs were growing. He looked into the bushes, beneath the branches, and sure enough, he located a small cricket. His friend was utterly amazed.

"That's incredible," said his friend. "You must have superhuman ears!"

"No," said the Native American. "My ears are no different from yours. It all depends on what you're listening for."

"But that can't be!" said the friend. "I could never hear a cricket in this noise."

"Yes, it's true," came the reply. "It depends on what is really important to you. Here, let me show you." He reached into his pocket, pulled out a few coins, and carefully dropped them on the sidewalk. And then, with the noise of the crowded street still blaring in their ears, they noticed every head within 20 feet turn and look to see if the money that had tinkled on the pavement was theirs.

"See what I mean?" said the Native American. "It all depends on what's important to you."

有的人由顺境塑造，另一些人则由逆境塑造。

——伊丽莎白·鲍恩

　　一个印第安人正和他的朋友一起在纽约市中心曼哈顿的时代广场附近走着。那时正是午餐时间，街上挤满了人。

　　汽车鸣着喇叭，出租车在拐弯处发出刺耳的声音，警笛呼啸着，城市的喧闹声几乎震耳欲聋。这时那个印第安人突然说："我听见一只蟋蟀在叫。"

他的朋友说："什么？你一定疯了，周围这么多噪声，你不可能听见蟋蟀叫！"

"我没疯，我确实是听到了，"印第安人说，"我听见一只蟋蟀的叫声。"

"别傻了。"朋友说。

印第安人侧耳听了一会儿，然后走到马路对面，来到一个种着灌木的大型水泥槽前。他在灌木中搜寻，在树枝下面，他果然找到了一只小蟋蟀。他的朋友非常吃惊。

"真难以置信，"他朋友说，"你一定有一对顺风耳！"

"不是，"印第安人说，"我的耳朵与你的没什么不同，这只是取决于你想听什么声音。"

"但那是不可能的！"朋友说，"在这些喧闹声中，我怎么也不可能听到蟋蟀的叫声。"

"真的能听到，"他回答说。"这取决于你认为什么是最重要的。来，我试给你看。"他伸手从口袋中拿出几枚硬币，悄悄地将它们扔到人行道上。然后，在熙熙攘攘的马路上噪音依然不绝于耳的情况下，他们看到在二十英尺范围内的每个人都回过头来，看看掉在路面上叮当响着的钱是不是他们的。

"明白我的意思了吧。"印第安人说道，"你能听到什么取决于你认为什么最重要。"

词汇识记

suddenly ['sʌdnli] *adv.* 突然地
例：Suddenly he began to scream loudly.
突然他开始大声尖叫起来。

carefully ['kɛə(r)fəli] *adv.* 小心地，仔细地

例：As long as you drive carefully, you will be very safe.

如果你开车小心，你就会很安全。

branch [brɑ:ntʃ] *n.* 分部，分店，分支，树枝

例：The gardener cut off a branch from the tree.

园丁从树上砍下一根树枝。

incredible [ɪnˈkredəbl] *adj.* 难以置信的，惊人的

例：I think it's incredible.

我认为这是难以置信的。

短语搭配

My ears are no different from yours.

be different from: 不同于

造句：_____

It all depends on what you're listening for.

depend on: 依赖，依靠，取决于，随……而定

造句：_____

译展身手

那时正是午餐时间，街上挤满了人。

译：_____

他的朋友非常吃惊。

译：_____

这取决于你认为什么是最重要的。

译：_____

Don't Step Out of Character
演好自己的角色

I am a slow walker, but I never walk backwards.

—Abraham Lincoln

On a plane flying from Chicago to New York, my seat companion was a young girl who gave me a friendly smile as I sat beside her, but whose young face showed great sadness. Hesitantly, she told me she was on her way to the funeral of her seventeen-year-old brother, who had been killed in Korea. She also told me that her only other relatives were two brothers, both in the service, and that they had lost their eldest brother in the war in Europe. I wanted to say something to comfort her... I felt so useless... All I could say was "I'm so sorry." And I thought, "Just what can I do to help bring order and hope into the world today?" And the thought came to me, "I can pray and my prayers will tune in with other sincere prayers to create a mighty force for good and for peace in the world."

As a girl I was fortunate in having old-fashioned, religious parents, and I often think of the old hymn my good father sang as stood beside him in church, "I need Thee every hour." As I've grown older my philosophy has changed in a way. I don't think of God now as an old man with a long gray beard sitting up on a throne. I believe in a practical religion. What good is it unless I can use it to help solve my daily problems, large or small?

I am grateful for what I consider the most worthwhile things in my life—a happy marriage, a good husband, and a son and daughter who become infinitely finer as they grow up. Success in my career has come second to these. However, no matter what my material blessings may be, I realize that my happiness must come from within myself. I can't get back anything I don't give out. Anybody knows a sure cure for the blues is to get out and do something nice for someone else.

I have had a wonderful opportunity on my tours to meet fine, good people in every one of the seven hundred towns I've played. I love my work. I believe that laughter is a great soul cleanser, and I pray that my audiences may somehow be better off for having seen my show. I believe in blessing everything and everybody along the way. Sometimes I may have let stage fright and nerves rob me and my audience of my best performance. I have failed if I haven't beforehand blessed everyone in my audience, everyone backstage. I admire their courage, their goodhearted generous qualities.

What do I mean by "blessing"? Well, I first have a deep sense of gratitude to an audience, and a feeling of good will and good wishes, so that I know there is complete harmony between them and me, and I know they will like me because I really like them—that we will tune in together.

My late brother, the great character actor and comedian, Charles "Chic" Sale, said to me one time we were talking about spiritual things and about being perfect channels for expression: "The thing to do is to stay in character—be God's child." And I try never to forget this.

我走得很慢，但是我从来不会后退。

——亚伯拉罕·林肯

　　一次，在从芝加哥飞往纽约的航班上，我坐在一个年轻女孩旁边。我坐下时她对我友好地笑了一下，但她年轻的面孔却流露出深切的悲痛。迟疑中，她向我道出了原委——她此行是要去参加她弟弟的葬礼，弟弟只有17岁，葬身在朝鲜战场。她的另两位兄弟是她仅有的亲人，都在服役，而她的大哥也已战死在欧洲。我很想安慰她……我觉得自己无能为力……只能对她说："我很难过。"我想，为了世界有太平和希望，我能做什么呢？突然我想到了祷告。"我可以祷告，我的祷告与其他虔诚的祷告一定能汇聚成一股巨大的力量，让世界充满美好与和平。"

　　我是个幸运的女孩，父母的思想很传统，笃信宗教。我常记起儿时在教堂里，站在我身边的父亲经常哼唱一首古老的赞美诗，"上帝啊，我时时刻刻需要你！"长大以后我的人生信条在某种程度上有所改变。我不再认为上帝是一个坐在宝座上、留着长长白胡子的老头。

我奉行的人生信条很现实。如果它不能帮我解决日常生活中大大小小的问题，那它有什么用呢？

对我来说，演艺事业的成功是次要的。人生最重要的是美满的婚姻、一个好丈夫和一双越来越有出息的子女。这些我都得到了，对此我心存感激。可是，无论我得到什么物质上的恩赐，真正的幸福必须源自我的内心。没有对他人的付出就不可能有任何回报。众所周知，随时准备行善才是根除忧愁的良药。

我的个人巡回演出给了我一个大好机会，使我结识了我所到的七百多个小镇上无数善良的人们。我热爱我的工作。我相信欢笑能净化灵魂，我祈祷我的演出能让人们更加幸福快乐。我相信我一路上给每件事每个人送去的祝福。有时我可能怯场、紧张，无法向观众呈现最精彩的表演。我演砸了是因为没有事先为每位观众、每位后台的工作人员祈福。他们都那么勇敢、善良、慷慨，令我钦佩不已。

我所说的"祈福"是什么意思呢？我首先对观众充满深深感激，然后对他们满怀美好的祝愿。这样一来我就知道我能和观众和谐互动，因为我真的喜爱他们，他们也会喜爱我——这样我们就能产生心灵的共鸣。

我已去世的哥哥查尔斯·"奇克"·塞尔是一位了不起的性格演员和喜剧演员。有一次我们谈起精神世界的话题，讨论完美的演技。我记得他对我说，"小家伙，做上帝的子民——这就是你要演好的角色"——这一点，我要努力永远铭记在心。

词汇识记

practical ['præktɪkəl] *adj.* 明智的，实际的，实用的

例：The whole scheme began to take on a more practical aspect.

整个计划开始具有更切合实际的性质。

worthwhile ['wə:θ'waɪl] *adj.* 值得(做)的

例：You'd better spend your time on some worthwhile reading.

你最好把时间花在读一些有价值的书上。

admire [əd'maɪə(r)] *v.* 钦佩，赞美，羡慕

例：You may not like him, but you have got to admire his persistence.

你可以不喜欢他，但你不得不佩服他那种坚韧不拔的精神。

短语搭配

As I've grown older my philosophy has changed in a way.

in a way: 在某种程度上

造句：＿＿＿＿＿＿＿＿＿＿＿＿＿＿＿＿＿＿＿＿＿＿＿

I can't get back anything I don't give out.

give out: 分发，散发，公布

造句：＿＿＿＿＿＿＿＿＿＿＿＿＿＿＿＿＿＿＿＿＿＿＿

译展身手

对我来说，演艺事业的成功是次要的。

译：＿＿＿＿＿＿＿＿＿＿＿＿＿＿＿＿＿＿＿＿＿＿＿

没有对他人的付出就不可能有任何回报。

译：＿＿＿＿＿＿＿＿＿＿＿＿＿＿＿＿＿＿＿＿＿＿＿

随身携带心灵的"调节器"
Carrying "Regulators" in Their Hearts

漫漫人生路，难免会有让人沮丧的时候。

不要轻言放弃，给自己留点时间做做梦，充一下电，这样你就能以崭新的面貌去面对每一天。

多想想美好的事情，用积极的提醒来提升你的乐观。

你可以写下一些短小的话语，并把它们放在你每天都会看到的地方，比如卫生间的镜子上、柜子里，或是电脑显示器上，以此来激励自己：

"我总有选择的余地。"

"我唯一能掌控的就是我对生活的态度。"

"我会看到每一件事情积极的一面，并让我的乐观情绪发光。"

Everyday Is a Gift
珍惜每一天

Do you love life? Then do not squander time; for that's the stuff life is made of.

—Benjamin Franklin

My brother in law opened the bottom drawer of my sister's bureau and lifted out a tissue-wrapped package. "This," he said, "is not a slip. This is lingerie."He discarded the tissue and handed me the slip.

It was exquisite, silk, handmade and trimmed with a cobweb of lace. The price tag with an astronomical figure on it was still attached.

"Jan bought this the first time we went to New York, at least 8 or 9 years ago. She never wore it. She was saving it for a special occasion."

Well, I guess this is the occasion.

He took the slip from me and put it on the bed, with the other clothes we were taking to the mortician. His hands lingered on the soft material for a moment, then he slammed the drawer shut and turned to me, "Don't ever save anything for a special occasion. Every day you're alive is a special occasion." I remembered those words through the funeral and the days that followed when I helped him and my niece attend to all the sad chores that follow an unexpected death. I thought about them on the plane returning to California from the midwestern town where my sister's family lives. I thought about all the things that she hadn't seen or heard or done. I thought about the things that she had done without realizing that they were special.

I'm still thinking about his words, and they've changed the weeds in the garden. I'm spending more time with my family and friends and less time in commercial meetings. Whenever possible, life should be a pattern of experience to savour, not endurance dure. I'm trying to recognize these moments now and cherish them. I'm not "saving" anything; we use our good china and crystal for every special event such as losing a pound, getting the sink unstopped, the first camellia blossom... I wear my good blazer to the market if I feel like it. My theory is if I look prosperous, I can shell out $ 28. 49 for one small bag of groceries without wincing. I'm not saving my good perfume for special parties; clerks in hardware stores and tellers in banks have noses that function as well as my party going friends.

"Someday" and "one of these days" are losing their grip on my vocabulary. If it's worth seeing or hearing or doing, I want to see and hear and do it now. I'm not sure what my sister would have done had she known that she wouldn't be here for the tomorrow we all take for granted. I think she would have called family members and a few close friends. She might have called a few former friends to apologize, and mend fences for past squabbles. I like to think she would have gone out for a Chinese dinner, her favorite food. I'm guessing. I'll never know.

It's those little things left undone that would make me angry if I knew that my hours were limited. Angry because I put off seeing good friends whom I was going to get in touch with someday. Angry because

I hadn't written certain letters that I intended to write one of these days. Angry and sorry that I didn't tell my husband and daughter often enough how much I truly love them.

I'm trying very hard not to put off, hold back, or save anything that would add laughter and luster to our lives. And every morning when I open my eyes, I tell myself that every day, every minute, every breath truly, is... a gift from God.

你热爱生命吗? 那么, 别浪费时间, 因为生命是由时间组成的。

——本杰明·富兰克林

妹夫打开了妹妹衣柜最底层抽屉, 拿出一个用纸包装的包裹。"这个, "他说, "不是件普通内衣, 而是一件豪华内衣。"他把薄纸撕开, 递给了我那件内衣。

它的确精致无比, 丝质、全手工缝制, 周围还有一圈网状蕾丝花边。价签都尚未拆去, 上面的数字高得惊人。

"这是我们第一次去纽约时买的, 至少已是八九年前的事了。她从没有穿过它。她想等一个特殊的日子再穿它。"

唉, 我想现在便是那特殊的日子了。

妹夫从我手中拿过内衣放在床上，和其他我们要带给殡仪服务人员的衣服放在一起。他的手在那柔软织物上徘徊了一会儿，随即砰的一声关上抽屉，转身对我说："永远不要把任何东西留给什么特殊日子。你活着的每一天就是一个特殊的日子。"这两句话久久在我耳边回响着，伴我度过了葬礼和帮妹夫、侄女处理妹妹意外死亡后的伤心后事的那几天。我从地处中西部的妹妹家返回加州时，在飞机上还是在想这两句话。我想到妹妹未曾有机会看到、听到或去做的事。我想到她淡然做过，但却没有意识到其特殊性的事。

我至今还在想着妹夫说的话，正是它们改变了我的心境。我花了更多的时间与家人朋友在一起，而少花些时间在那些工作会议上。无论何时，生活应当是一种"品味"而非一种"忍受"。我在学习欣赏每一刻，并珍惜每一刻。我不再去"珍藏"任何东西；只要有一点好事，我们就不吝啬使用精美的瓷器和水晶制品，比如说当体重减了一磅时，当厨房水槽堵塞通了时，当第一朵山茶花绽放时……如果我想穿，我就穿上我的名牌衣服去市场购物。我的理论是：如果我看上去还富足的话，我可以毫不心疼地为一小袋杂货付出28.49美元。我不再为特殊的派对而珍藏我上好的香水；五金店售货员和银行出纳员们的嗅觉，不会比派对上的朋友们来得差。

"有朝一日"和"终有一天"这样的词正从我的常用词汇中淡出。如果值得去看、去听或去做，我当即就要去看、去听或去做。人们总是理所当然地以为自己必然有明天，不知假如妹妹知道她将没有明日，她会做些什么。我想她会给家人和几位密友打电话。她可能还会给几位昔日朋友打电话主动道歉，摒弃前嫌。我想她可能会外出吃顿她喜欢的中餐。我只是猜想而已。我永远也不会知道。

假如我知道我的时间不多了，那些没来得及做的小事会让我恼火。恼火是因为我一拖再拖没能去看看"有朝一日"会去看的好友们。恼火是因为我还没有写出我"终有一天"要写的信。恼火与内疚是因为我没能更经常地告诉我的丈夫和女儿：我是多么真切地爱他们。

我正努力不再拖延——保留或珍藏那些能给我们生活带来欢笑和光彩的东西。每天清晨当我睁开双眼，我便告诉自己每一天、每一分钟、每一瞬间都真是……上帝赐予的礼物。

词汇识记

occasion [əˈkeɪʒn] *n.* 时刻，场合
例：I've met her on several occasions recently.
我最近见到过她好几次。

prosperous [ˈprɒspərəs] *adj.* 繁荣的，兴旺的
例：At no time has the country been more prosperous than at present.
我国任何时候都没有现在这样繁荣。

apologize [əˈpɒlədʒaɪz] *v.* 道歉，认错，谢罪
例：You must apologize to your sister for being so rude.
你太无理了，必须向你姐姐道歉。

angry ['æŋgrɪ] *adj.* 发怒的，愤怒的，生气的

例：Don't be angry over such trivial matters.

别为这些琐事生气。

短语搭配

Jan bought this the first time we went to New York.

the first time: 第一次

造句：＿＿＿＿＿＿＿＿＿＿＿＿＿＿＿＿＿＿＿＿

I wear my good blazer to the market if I feel like it.

feel like: 想要

造句：＿＿＿＿＿＿＿＿＿＿＿＿＿＿＿＿＿＿＿＿

译展身手

永远不要把任何东西留给什么特殊日子。你活着的每一天就是一个特殊的日子。

译：＿＿＿＿＿＿＿＿＿＿＿＿＿＿＿＿＿＿＿＿

假如我知道我的时间不多了，那些没来得及做的小事会让我恼火。

译：＿＿＿＿＿＿＿＿＿＿＿＿＿＿＿＿＿＿＿＿

我便告诉自己每一天、每一分钟、每一瞬间都真是……上帝赐予的礼物。

译：＿＿＿＿＿＿＿＿＿＿＿＿＿＿＿＿＿＿＿＿

To Give Up Is Also a Kind of Wisdom
敢于放弃也是一种智慧

I can accept failure, but I can't accept not trying.

—Michael Jordan

There once was a master who went to India. In those times, we didn't have the communications or airplanes or many kinds of transportation as we do now. So the master went to India on foot. He had never been to India before; perhaps he came from Persia. And when he got there, he saw a lot of fruit. In India they have plenty of fruit to sell, but much of it is expensive because they can't grow much due to the water situation. So he saw one basket—a big basket of some very red, long fruit. And it was the cheapest in the shop, not expensive at all.

So he went up and asked, "How much per kilo?" And the shopkeeper said, "Two rupees." Two rupees in India is nothing; it's like dirt. So he bought a whole kilogram of the fruit and started eating it. But after he ate some of it: Oh, my God! His eyes watered, his mouth watered and burned, his eyes were burning, his head was burning and his face became red. As he coughed and choked and gasped for breath, he jumped up and down, saying, "Ah! Ah! Ah!"

But he still continued to eat the fruit! Some people who were looking at him shook their heads and said, "You're crazy, man. Those are chilies! You can't eat so many; they're not good for you! People use them as a condiment, but only a little bit to put into food for taste. You can't just eat them by the handful like that; they're not fruit!" So the stupid master said, "No, I can't stop! I paid money for them, and now I'll eat them. It's my money!"

And you think that master was stupid, right? Similarly, we sometimes do a lot of things like that. We invest money, time or effort in a relationship, business or job. And even though it's been a long time, bitter experience tells us it won't work, and we know there's no more hope that things will change in the future—which we definitely know by intuition—we still continue just because we've invested money, time, effort and love into it. If so, we're kaput in the brain. Just like the man who ate the chilies and suffered so much but couldn't stop because he didn't want to waste the money he'd paid.

So even if you've lost something, let it go and move on. That's better than continuing to lose.

我可以接受失败，但我不能接受放弃！

——迈克尔·乔丹

　　从前有一位师父，他到印度去，那时候因为交通不发达，没有飞机，不像现在一样有很多交通工具，所以这位师父就步行去印度。他有可能是波斯人，以前没去过印度。他到达印度时，看见许许多多的水果。在印度，有时因为缺水的缘故，水果产量不多，许多小店虽然摆满了水果，但多半都很贵。那位师父发现有个大篮子里面装着一种红色长条形的水果，这种水果的价格最便宜，一点都不贵。

　　他就走过去询问："这个一公斤要多少钱？"小贩回答："两卢比。"两卢比在印度根本不算什么，像尘土一样不值钱，于是他就整整买了一公斤，然后开始吃。吃了几口之后，这位师父就眼泪、口水齐流，眼睛发红，嘴巴辣得像着火一样，整个头好像要烧起来，他又咳又呛，满脸通红地喘不过气来，在那里边跳边叫："啊！啊！啊！"

　　不过他还是继续吃！有人看到他这样子后，就摇摇头说："老兄，你是脑袋坏掉啦？这是辣椒耶！不能吃那么多，这样对你不好。辣椒是用来调味的，煮菜时每次只放一点点在食物里增加味道。这个不是水果，不能这样整把拿起来吃啊！"那位笨师父说："不行，我已经花钱买了，就要把它吃完，这可都是钱哪！"

　　你们觉得这位师父很笨，是吗？其实我们有时候也做很多类似的傻事。有时候我们在某些感情或事业工作上，投入了金钱、时间和心力，经过长期的经营之后，我们从惨痛的经验中知道行不通，直觉也很清楚未来不会有任何转机，但我们还是舍不得放弃，因为已经投入了金钱、时间、心力和感情在里面。像这种情形，表示说我们头脑坏掉，就像那个吃辣椒的人一样，明明已经那么痛苦了，还是不肯停止，只因为不想白白浪费已经付出的钱。

　　就算你会有所损失，还是要放下，然后继续前进！这样总比一直损失下去来得好。

词汇识记

master ['mɑ:stə(r)] *n.* 大师，主人

例：The dog came bounding up to its master.

那狗蹿到主人面前。

choke [tʃəʊk] *v.* （使）窒息，呛；塞满

例：She choked (to death) on a fish bone.

鱼刺把她卡住而导致她窒息（而死）。

condiment ['kɒndɪmənt] *n.* 调味品

例：I just don't like being compared to a condiment.

我只是不想跟调料做比较。

suffer ['sʌfə(r)] *v.* 遭受；容忍；受痛苦；受损，变糟

例：How can you suffer such insolence?

你怎么能容忍这种蛮横的态度？

短语搭配

So the master went to India on foot.

on foot: 步行

造句：_____

As he coughed and choked and gasped for breath, he jumped up and

down, saying,"Ah! Ah! Ah!"

jump up and down: 跳上跳下

造句：_____

If so, we're kaput in the brain.

if so: 如果是这样的话

造句：_____

译展身手

这种水果的价格最便宜，一点都不贵。

译：_____

就算你会有所损失，还是要放下，然后继续前进。

译：_____

Life Comes in a Package
有种旅行叫作人生

No one can degrade us except ourselves; that if we are worthy, no influence can defeat us.

—B. T. Washington

Life comes in a package. This package includes happiness and sorrow, failure and success, hope and despair. Life is a learning process. Experiences in life teach us new lessons and make us a better person. With each passing day we learn to handle various situations.

Love

Love plays a pivotal role on our life. Love makes you feel wanted. Without love a person could go hayward and also become cruel and ferocious. In the early stage of our life, our parents are the ones who shower us with unconditional love and care, and teach us about what is right and wrong, good and bad. But we always tend to take this for granted. It is only after marriage and having kids that a person understands and becomes sensitive to others' feelings. Kids make a person responsible and mature and help us to understand life better.

Happiness and Sorrow

Materialistic happiness is short-lived, but happiness achieved by

bringing a smile on others face gives a certain level of fulfillment. Peace of mind is the main link to happiness. No mind is happy without peace. We realize the true worth of happiness when we are in sorrow. Sorrow is basically due to death of a loved one, failure and despair. But these things are temporary and will pass away.

Failure and Success

Failure is the path to success. It helps us to touch the sky, teaches us to survive and shows us a specific way. Success brings in money, fame, pride and self-respect. Here it becomes very important to keep our head on our shoulder. The only way to show our gratitude to God for bestowing success on us is by being humble, modest, courteous and respectful to the less fortunate ones.

Hope and Despair

Hope is what keeps life going. Parents always hope their children will do well. Hope makes us dream. Hope builds in patience. Life teaches us not to despair even in the darkest hour, because after every night there is a day. Nothing remains the same. We have only one choice keep moving on in life and be hopeful.

Life teaches us not to regret over yesterday, for it has passed and is beyond our control. Tomorrow is unknown, for it could either be bright or dull. So the only alternative is work hard today, so that we will enjoy a better tomorrow.

除了我们自己以外，没有人能贬低我们。如果我们坚强，就没有什
么不良影响能够打败我们。

——B.T.华盛顿

人生好似一个包裹，这个包裹里藏着快乐与悲伤、成功与失败、
希望与绝望。人生也是一个学习的过程。那些经历给我们上了全新的
课，让我们变得更好。随着每一天的过去，我们学会了处理各种各样
的问题。

爱

爱在生活之外扮演了一个关键的角色。爱使你想要得到些什么。
没有爱，一个人将走向不归路，变得凶暴、残忍。在我们最初的人生
道路上，我们的父母给予了我们无条件的关爱，他们教会我们判断正
确与错误、好与坏。然而我们常常把这想当然了，只有等到我们结了
婚并且有了孩子之后，一个人才会懂得并注意别人的感受。孩子让我
们变得富有责任心、变得成熟稳重，并且更好地理解人生。

快乐与悲伤

物质上的快乐往往是短暂的，然而，当你给予他人一个微笑的

时候，那种满足却是无与伦比的。心灵的平静往往是快乐的源泉。没有平和的心态就没有快乐的心情。在伤心的时候，我们往往能够体会到快乐的真谛。悲伤基本都来自于一个爱人的去世、失败，还有绝望，但是这样的事情都是暂时的，总会过去的。

失败与成功

失败是成功之母。它让我们触及蓝天，它教会我们如何生存，它给予我们一条特殊的路。成功给予我们金钱、名誉、骄傲和自尊。这里，保持头脑清醒便显得尤为重要。唯一能让我们感激上帝给予的成功便是始终卑微、谦虚、礼貌，并且尊重没有我们幸运的人们。

希望与绝望

希望是人生动力之源。父母总是希望自己的孩子能够做得很好。希望使我们有梦想。希望使我们变得有耐心。人生教会我们即使是在最困难的时候都不要绝望，因为黑暗之后终将是黎明。没有什么是一成不变的，我们唯有充满希望地继续生活。

人生教会我们不要对过去的事感到后悔，因为过去的终究是过去了并且我们已无法控制。没人知道明天会是怎样，因为它可以是光明的，同样也可以是无趣的。所以，唯一的选择便是在今天努力工作，这样才能让我们去享受更美好的明天。

词汇识记

include [ɪnˈkluːd] v. 包括，包含

例：The traditional breakfast in this area includes bacon and eggs.

这个地区传统的早饭包括火腿和鸡蛋。

process ['prəʊses] *n.* 过程，进程
例：Producing a dictionary is a slow process.
编成一本字典是一个缓慢的过程。

handle ['hændl] *v.* 处理，应付
例：I was impressed by her handling of the affair.
我觉得她对此事的处理很了不起。

sensitive ['sensətɪv] *adj.* 灵敏的，敏感的，感光的，易受伤害的，善解人意的
例：He is too sensitive to criticism.
他对批评太敏感。

短语搭配

Love plays a pivotal role on our life.
play a pivotal role: 起着举足轻重的作用
造句：_____

Success brings in money, fame, pride and self-respect.
bring in: 介绍；带进，引进
造句：_____

译展身手

那些经历给我们上了全新的课，让我们变得更好。
译：_____
失败是成功之母。
译：_____

The Missing Blessing
错过的祝福

As selfishness and complaint cloud the mind, so love with its joy clears and sharpens the vision.

—Helen Keller

A young man was getting ready to graduate from college. For many months he had admired a beautiful sports car in a dealer's showroom, and knowing his father could afford it, he told him that was all he wanted.

As the graduation day approached, the young man awaited signs that his father had purchased the car. Finally, on the morning of his graduation, his father called him into his private study. His father told him how proud he was to have such a fine son, and told him how much he loved him. He handed his son a beautiful wrapped gift box. Curious, but somewhat disappointed, the young man opened the box and found a *Bible*, with the young man's name embossed in gold. Angrily, he raised his voice to his father and said, "With all your money you give me a *Bible*?" He then stormed out of the house, leaving the *Bible*.

Many years passed and the young man was very successful in business. He had a beautiful home and a wonderful family, but realizing his father was very old, he thought perhaps he should go to see him. He had not seen him since that graduation day. Before he could make the arrangements, he received a telegram telling him his father had passed away, and willed all of his possessions to his son. He needed to come home immediately and take care of things.

When he arrived at his father's house, sudden sadness and regret filled his heart. He began to search through his father's important papers and saw the still new *Bible*, just as he had left it years ago. With tears, he opened the *Bible* and began to turn the pages. As he was reading, a car key dropped from the back of the *Bible*. It had a tag with the dealer's name, the same dealer who had the sports car he had desired. On the tag was the date of his graduation, and the words "PAID IN FULL."

How many times do we miss blessings because they are not packaged as we expected? Do not spoil what you have by desiring what you have not; but remember that what you now have was once among the things you only hoped for.

Sometimes we don't realize the good fortune we have or we could have because we expect "the packaging" to be different. What may appear as bad fortune may in fact be the door that is just waiting to be opened.

自私和抱怨是心灵的阴暗，愉快的爱则使视野明朗开阔。

——海伦·凯勒

从前，有位年轻人即将大学毕业。数月来，他一直渴望得到某汽车商产品陈列室中的一辆跑车。他知道他父亲肯定买得起这辆车，于是他便跟父亲说他很想得到那辆漂亮的跑车。

毕业典礼即将来临，年轻人等待着父亲买下跑车的消息。终于，在毕业典礼那天上午，父亲将他叫到自己的书房。父亲告诉他，有他这么出色的儿子自己感到非常自豪而且非常爱他这个儿子。接着，父亲递给儿子一个包装精美的礼品盒。年轻人感到好奇，但带着些许失望地打开礼品盒，却发现里面是一本精美的精装本《圣经》，上面以金字凸印着年轻人的名字。看罢，年轻人怒气冲冲地向父亲大喊道："你有那么多钱，却只给我一本《圣经》？"说完，便丢下《圣经》，愤怒地冲出房子。

多年以后，年轻人已事业有成。他拥有一所漂亮的房子，和一个温馨的家庭，但他意识到父亲年事已高，或许应该去看看他。自从毕业那天起他就一直不见父亲。就在起程时，他收到一封电报——父亲已逝世，并已立下遗嘱将其所有财产转给儿子。他要立即回父亲家处理后事。

当到了父亲的房子里时，他内心突然感到一阵悲伤与懊悔。他开始仔细搜寻父亲的重要文件，突然发现了那本《圣经》——还跟几年前一样崭新。噙着泪水，他打开《圣经》并一页一页地阅读着。忽然，从书的背面掉出一把钥匙。钥匙上挂着一个标签，上面写着一个汽车经销商的名字——正是他曾渴望的那辆跑车的经销商。标签上还有他的毕业日期及"款已付清"的字样。

我们多少次与祝福擦肩而过，仅仅因为它们没有按我们想象中的样子包装好？不要在渴望得到没有的东西时损坏你已经拥有的东西，但要记住一点：你现在所拥有的恰恰正是你曾经一心渴望得到的。

有时，我们并没有意识到我们已经拥有或本该拥有的好运，仅仅因为它的外表与我们想象中的有所不同。其实，表面上看起来像是坏运气的东西或许正是等待开启的幸运之门。

词汇识记

afford [əˈfɔːd] v. 给予；供应得起；提供
例：We can't afford to send our children to college.
我们不能负担得起送我们的孩子上大学。

approach [əˈprəʊʃ] v. 靠近；接近
例：As I approached the house, I noticed a light on upstairs.
当我走进房子时，我注意到了楼上开着灯。

arrangement [əˈreɪndʒmənt] *n.* 布置，安排，约定

例：We have made all the arrangements for the conference.

我们已做好会议的全部筹备工作。

fortune [ˈfɔːtʃən] *n.* 财富，运气

例：He dreamed of making a fortune.

他梦想发大财。

短语搭配

A young man was getting ready to graduate from college.

graduate from: 毕业

造句：_____

Before he could make the arrangements, he received a telegram telling him his father had passed away...

pass away: 去世；消逝

造句：_____

He needed to come home immediately and take care of things.

take care of: 照顾；处理

造句：_____

译展身手

噙着泪水，他打开《圣经》并一页一页地阅读着。

译：_____

其实，表面上看起来像是坏运气的东西或许正是等待开启的幸运之门。

译：_____

Think Positively Every Day
积极看待每一天

We must accept finite disappointment, but we must never lose infinite hope.

—Mattin Luther King

If your life feels like it is lacking the power that you want and the motivation that you need, sometimes all you have to do is shift your point of view.

By training your thoughts to concentrate on the bright side of things, you are more likely to have the incentive to follow through on your goals. You are less likely to be held back by negative ideas that might limit your performance.

Your life can be enhanced, and your happiness enriched, when you choose to change your perspective. Don't leave your future to chance, or wait for things to get better mysteriously on their own. You must go in the direction of your hopes and aspirations. Begin to build your confidence, and work through problems rather than avoid them. Remember that power is not necessarily control over situations, but the ability to deal with whatever comes your way.

Always believe that good things are possible, and remember that mistakes can be lessons that lead to discoveries. Take your fear and transform it into trust; learn to rise above anxiety and doubt. Turn your "worry hours"into"productive hours". Take the energy that you have wasted and direct it toward every worthwhile effort that you can be involved in. You will see beautiful things happen when you allow yourself to experience the joys of life. You will find happiness when you adopt positive thinking into your daily routine and make it an important part of your world.

我们必须接受失望，因为它是有限的，但千万不可失去希望，因为它是无穷的。

——马丁·路德·金

如果你觉得心有余力不足，觉得缺乏前进的动力，有时候你只需要改变思维的角度。

试着训练自己的思想朝好的一面看，这样你就会汲取实现目标的动力，而不会因为消极沉沦停滞不前。

一旦变换看问题的角度，你的生活会豁然开朗，幸福快乐会接踵而来。别交出掌握命运的主动权，也别指望局面会不可思议地好转。你必须与内心希望与热情步调一致。建立自信，敢于与困难短兵相接，而非绕道而行。记住，力量不是驾驭局势的法宝，无坚不摧的能力才是最重要的。

　　请坚信，美好的降临并非不可能，失误也许是成功的前奏。将惶恐化作信任，学会超越担忧和疑虑。让"诚惶诚恐"的时光变得"富有成效"。不要挥霍浪费精力，而要将它投入到有意义的事情中去。当你下意识地品尝生命的欢愉时，美好就会出现。当你积极地看待生活，并以此作为你的日常准则时，你就会找到快乐的真谛。

lacking ['lækɪŋ] *adj.* 缺少的，没有的
例：She's not lacking in intelligence.
她并不缺乏学识。

negative ['negətɪv] *adj.* 消极的，负面的；否定的

例：Will it have any negative influence on other guys?

这是否会对其他人造成消极的影响？

worthwhile [ˌwəːθ'waɪl] *adj.* 值得（做）的

例：I don't think it worthwhile taking such trouble.

我想不值得费这么大的事了。

短语搭配

Begin to build your confidence, and work through problems rather than avoid them.

rather than: 与其……倒不如，不是……而是

造句：＿＿＿＿＿＿＿＿＿＿＿＿＿＿＿＿＿＿＿＿＿＿

Take your fear and transform it into trust.

transform into: 转变成

造句：＿＿＿＿＿＿＿＿＿＿＿＿＿＿＿＿＿＿＿＿＿＿

译展身手

记住，力量不是驾驭局势的法宝，无坚不摧的能力才是最重要的。

译：＿＿＿＿＿＿＿＿＿＿＿＿＿＿＿＿＿＿＿＿＿＿＿＿

请坚信，美好的降临并非不可能，失误也许是成功的前奏。

译：＿＿＿＿＿＿＿＿＿＿＿＿＿＿＿＿＿＿＿＿＿＿＿＿

Just for Today
就为了今天

The time of life is short; to spend that shortness basely, it would be too long.
—William Shakespeare

Just for today I will try to live through this day only and not tackle my whole life problem at once. I can do something for twelve hours that would appall me if I had to keep it up for a lifetime.

Just for today I will be happy. This assumes to be true what Abraham Lincoln said, that "Most folks are as happy as they make up their minds to be."

Just for today I will adjust myself to what is, and not try to adjust everything to my own desires. I will take my "luck" as it comes.

Just for today I will try to strengthen my mind. I will study. I will learn something useful. I will not be a mental loafer. I will read something that requires effort, thought and concentration.

Just for today I will exercise my soul in three ways. I will do somebody a good turn and not get found out: If anybody knows of it, it will not count. I will do at least two things I don't want to do—just for exercise. I will not show anyone that my feelings are hurt: they may be hurt, but today I will not show it.

Just for today I will be agreeable. I will look as well as I can, dress becomingly, talk low, act courteously, criticize not one bit, and try not to improve or regulate anybody but myself.

Just for today I will have a program, I may not follow it exactly, but I will have it. I will save myself from two pests: hurry and indecision.

Just for today I will have a quiet half hour all by myself and relax. During this half hour, sometime, I will try to get a better perspective of my life.

Just for today I will be unafraid. Especially I will not be afraid to enjoy what is beautiful, and to believe that as I give to the world, so the world will give to me.

人生苦短，若虚度年华，则短暂的人生就太长了。

——威廉·莎士比亚

就为了今天，我将尽力只度过今天而不立刻去解决终身的问题。对一件令我沮丧而又必须坚持一辈子的事，我只能坚持十二个小时。

就为了今天，我会很快乐。亚伯拉罕·林肯说过，"大多数人都是决定想怎么高兴就怎么高兴。"这已经被认为是真理。

就为了今天，我会做自我调整适应事物本来的面目，而不是想方设法使每一件事满足自己的欲望。当机会来临的时候我会抓住它。

就为了今天，我会尽力心强志坚。我会学习，学一些有用的东西。我不会做一个精神上的流浪汉。我会读一些需要努力、思考和注意力集中的东西。

就为了今天，我会用三种方法来磨炼我的灵魂。我会做对某人有利的事但不能被发现，若有人发现了就不算数。我将会做至少两件我不愿做的事情——只为了磨炼。我不会让任何人感到我的感情受到了伤害：它们可能受到了伤害，但今天我不想表现出来。

就为了今天，我会过得很惬意。看起来我达到了最佳状态，穿着得体、讲话谦虚、行为礼貌、一点不吹毛求疵，尽量改进和调节自己而不是别人。

就为了今天，我会制订一个计划，我也许不会严格地遵守它，但我一定要有计划。我会避免两种错误：仓促行事和优柔寡断。

就为了今天，我将会独自静静地待上半小时放松。在这半小时里，某个时刻，我会对我日后的生活有个更好的看法。

就为了今天，我将不再害怕。尤其我不会再害怕享受美丽的事物，并且相信我给予世界的，世界也会给予我。

词汇识记

adjust [əˈdʒʌst] *v.* 调整，调节，使适应

例：He can't adjust himself to the whirl of modern life in this big city.
他无法适应这个大都市的现代生活的忙碌。

strengthen ['streŋθən] *v.* 加强，巩固

例：He has been brought in to strengthen the defence.

已请他来加强后卫力量。

regulate ['regjuleɪt] *v.* 调整，调节；管理，控制

例：Can you regulate this watch so that it keeps time accurately?

你能不能调一下这块表，让它走得准一些？

relax [rɪ'læks] *v.* 放松，(使)松弛；放宽，缓和

例：The music will help to relax you.

音乐会使你感到轻松。

短语搭配

Most folks are as happy as they make up their minds to be.

make up one's mind: 下定决心，打定主意

造句：_____

I will do somebody a good turn and not get found out: If anybody knows of it, it will not count.

find out: 找出，查明，发现

造句：_____

译展身手

当机会来临的时候我会抓住它。

译：_____

就为了今天，我将不再害怕。

译：_____

Listening Is a Good Medicine
倾听是一剂良药

The thoughts that come often unsought, and, as it were, drop into the mind, are commonly the most valuable of any we have.

—John Locke

It was Sunday. I had one last patient to see. I approached her room in a hurry and stood at the doorway. She was an older woman, sitting at the edge of the bed, struggling to put socks on her swollen feet. I crossed the threshold, spoke quickly to the nurse, scanned her chart noting she was in stable condition.

I leaned on the bedrail looking down at her. She asked if I could help put on her socks. Instead, I launched into a monologue that went something like this: "How are you feeling? Your sugars and blood pressure were high but they're better today. The nurse mentioned you're anxious to see your son who's visiting you today. It's nice to have family visit from far away. I bet you really look forward to seeing him."

She stopped me with a stern voice. "Sit down, doctor. This is my story, not your story."

I was surprised and embarrassed. I sat down and helped her with the socks. She told me that her only son lived around the corner from her, but she had not seen him for five years. She believed that the stress of this contributed greatly to her health problems. After hearing her story and putting on her socks, I asked if there was anything else I could do for her. She shook her head and smiled. All she wanted me to do was to listen.

Each story is different. Some are detailed; others are vague. Some have a beginning, middle and end. Others wander without a clear conclusion. Some are true; others not. Yet all those things do not really matter. What matters to the storyteller is that the story is heard — without interruption, assumption or judgment.

I often thought of what that woman taught me, and I reminded myself of the importance of stopping, sitting down and truly listening. I believe in the power of listening. I know firsthand that immeasurable healing takes place within me when someone stops, sits down and listens to my story.

那些不期而至，仿佛从天而降的思想，通常是我们所有思想中最具有价值的部分。

——约翰·洛克

那是一个周日。我要去见最后一位病人。我匆匆忙忙地走向她的病房，站到了门口。病人是位老妇人，此时她正坐在床沿上努力为自己浮肿的双脚穿上袜子。我跨进屋，快速和护士进行了交流，然后看了看病人的病历表。根据表格上的记录，她目前状况稳定。

我倚在床栏上低头看着她。她问我是否可以帮她把袜子穿上。我没有回答，而是自顾自地说起来："你感觉怎么样？你的血糖和血压有点高，不过今天好多了。你的儿子今天要来看你，护士说你非常想见他。有家人远道来看望自己真是不错。我相信你真的很渴望见到他。"

她用一种严厉的口气将我打断："大夫，坐下来。这是我的事儿，不是你的。"

我既惊讶又尴尬。我坐了下来，帮她穿袜子。她告诉我，她的独生子就住在她家附近，但她已经有五年没见到儿子了。她相信，这件事给她的压力很大程度上加重了她的病情。听完她的故事并帮她穿上袜子后，我问她我还能为她做些什么。她摇了摇头，然后笑了起来。她要让我做的全部事情就是听她讲故事。

每个故事都是不同的。有些故事详细，有些却模糊；有些故事有开始、经过和结果，有些则天马行空，没有明确的结论；有些故事是真实的，而有些不是。不过，这些要素都不是最重要的。对讲述者来说，真正重要的是，这个故事要有人去倾听——不要打断，不要臆断，也不要去评价。

我跟他们说，我相信倾听是味良药。我亲身体会到，当有人停下自己的事，坐下来聆听你的故事时，会在你的身体里产生无法估量的治愈力。

词汇识记

launch [lɔ:ntʃ] *v.* 发起，推出（新产品）

例：The ship launched in the direction of Japan.

船起航前往日本。

contribute [kən'trɪbjuːt] *v.* 投稿，贡献，是……的原因之一

例：Snacks are generally high in calories and may contribute to weight gain.

小零食一般都含有很高的热量，很容易导致发胖。

conclusion [kən'kluːʒn] *n.* 结尾，结论

例：Your information is inaccurate and your conclusion is therefore wrong.

你的信息不准确，所以你的结论是错误的。

interruption [ˌɪntəˈrʌpʃən] *n.* 打岔，中断
例：He was impatient of any interruption.
他对任何打扰都感到不耐烦。

短语搭配

I approached her room in a hurry and stood at the doorway.

in a hurry: 匆忙

造句：_____

I bet you really look forward to seeing him.

look forward to: 期望；盼望

造句：_____

I know firsthand that immeasurable healing takes place within me.

take place: 发生；举行

造句：_____

译展身手

有家人远道来看望自己真是不错。

译：_____

她要让我做的全部事情就是听她讲故事。

译：_____

生命的出口
The Export of Life

有些人坚持认为只有今日和明日才是重要的，可是今日我们做的许多事是徒劳不足取的，很快就会被忘记，许多我们期待明天将要做的事却从来没有发生过。

生命不是一场赛跑，而是一步一个脚印的旅程。

　　当你身陷困境的时候，回想你生命中快乐和幸福的时刻，回想它是如何使你快乐的。

　　这样，你就会发现你有能力克服每个障碍，你便有了走出困境的勇气。

　　从你的生活中多抽出点时间去梦想，重振你的精力，你会完全准备好又去迎接新的一天。

　　别为生活找借口，活在当下，努力在当下。

The Rainbow Is a Sign of Hope for Tomorrow
彩虹是明日希望的象征

Each moment in history is a fleeting time, precious and unique.

—Richard Nixon

Once upon a time the colors of the world started to quarrel. All claimed that they were the best.

Green said: "Clearly I am the most important. I am the sign of life and of hope. I was chosen for grass, trees and leaves. Look over the countryside and you will see that I am in the majority."

Blue interrupted: "You only think about the earth, but consider the sky and the sea. It is the water that is the basis of life. The sky gives space and peace and serenity. Without my peace, you would all be nothing."

Yellow chuckled: " The sun is yellow, the moon is yellow, the stars are yellow. Every time you look at a sunflower, the whole world starts to smile. Without me there would be no fun."

Orange started next: "I carry the most important vitamins. Think of carrots, oranges and mangoes. When I fill the sky at sunrise or sunset, my beauty is so striking that no one gives another thought to any of you."

Red could stand it no longer so he shouted out: "I am the ruler of all of you. I am blood—life's blood! I bring fire into the blood. I am the color of passion and love."

Purple was very tall and spoke with great pomp: "I am the color of royalty and power. Kings, chiefs and bishops have always chosen me for I am the sign of authority and wisdom. People do not question me! They listen and obey."

Finally indigo spoke, much more quietly than all the others, but with just as much determination: "Think of me. I am the color of silence. I represent thought and reflection, twilight and deep water. You need me for balance and contrast, for prayer and inner peace."

And so the colors went on quarreling, each convinced of his or her own superiority. Suddenly there was a startling flash of bright lightening, and thunder rolled. Rain started to pour down.

Rain began to speak: "You foolish colors. Don't you know that you were each made for a special purpose? Join hands with one another and come to me."

Doing as they were told, the colors joined hands and united.

Rain continued: "From now on, when it rains, each of you will stretch across the sky in a great bow of color as a reminder that you can all live in peace. The rainbow is a sign of hope for tomorrow."

历史巨轮飞转，分分秒秒的时间都十分宝贵，也独具意义。

——理查德·尼克松

有一天，世界上的五颜六色彼此争吵了起来，每一个颜色都声称自己是最好的。

绿色说："很明显嘛！我就是最重要的。我是生命和希望的象征。青草、大树和叶子都选择我，只要往乡野望去，我就是主色。"

蓝色打断他的话说："你只想到地面，想想天空和海洋吧！水是生命之源，而天空包容大地、宁静和祥和。一旦失去我的宁静祥和，你们就什么也不是了。"

黄色暗自好笑："太阳是黄色的，月亮是黄色的，星星也是黄色的。每当你看着向日葵，整个世界也跟着笑逐颜开起来。没有了我，也就没有了乐趣。"

橙色接着说："我是最重要的维生素，想想胡萝卜、橘子和芒果。每当日出日落时，我就满布在天空，我的美丽如此令人惊艳，根本不会有人想到你们。"

红色再也按捺不住，他大声地说："我是你们的主宰，我是血！生命之血！我将热情注入血液，我是热情和爱情的颜色。"

紫色自视甚高，而且盛气凌人地说："我是皇室和权威的颜色，国王、领袖和大主教都选择我，因为我是权威和智慧的象征。人们不敢对我有所存疑，只有乖乖听命的份。"

靛色终于说话了，比起其他颜色，他的声音平和多了，但是，也是同样的斩钉截铁："我是宁静之声，我代表思想、深思熟虑、曙光以及深水。你们需要我来平衡对比、祈祷并获得内在的平静。"

五颜六色就这样一直吵下去，每个颜色都认为自己最优秀。突然间闪电雷鸣大作，大雨倾盆而下。

雨开口说话："你们这些蠢颜色，你们不晓得自己各有所司吗？大家手牵手一起过来。"

那些颜色都乖乖地手牵手，站在一起。

雨接着说："从今以后，只要一下雨，你们每个都得伸展成大弓形横跨在天际，借以提醒大家和平共处。因为彩虹是明日希望的象征。"

词汇识记

interrupt [ˌɪntəˈrʌpt] *v.* 打断，打扰

例：His telephone call interrupted my train of thought.

他的电话打断了我的思路。

vitamin [ˈvɪtəmɪn] *n.* 维生素

例：The bread is fortified with various vitamins.

这种面包加有各种维生素。

represent [ˌreprɪˈzent] *v.* 代表(理)；表示，象征

例：The rose represents England.

玫瑰花是英格兰的象征。

quarrel [ˈkwɒrəl] *v.* 争吵；反对，挑剔

例：I would rather be laughed at than quarrel with him.

我宁愿被嘲笑，也不愿和他吵架。

短语搭配

Red could stand it no longer so he shouted out: "I am the ruler of all of you."

no longer: 不再，已不

造句：_____

shout out: 大声喊叫……

造句：_____

Rain started to pour down.

pour down:（雨）倾盆而下

造句: _____

From now on, when it rains, ... that you can all live in peace.

from now on: 从现在起，今后

造句: _____

译展身手

只要往乡野望去，我就是主色。

译: _____

没有了我，也就没有了乐趣。

译: _____

那些颜色都乖乖地手牵手，站在一起。

译: _____

Youth
青　春

Try not to become a man of success but rather try to become a man of value.

—A. Einstein

Man's youth is a wonderful thing: it is so full of anguish and of magic and he never comes to know it as it is, until it has gone from him forever. It is the thing he cannot bear to lose, it is the thing whose passing he watches with infinite sorrow and regret, it is the thing whose loss with a sad and secret joy, the thing he would never willingly relive again, could it be restored to him by any magic.

Why is this? The reason is that the strange and bitter miracle of life is nowhere else so evident as in our youth. And what is the essence of that strange and bitter miracle of life which we feel so poignant, so unutterable, with such a bitter pain and joy, when we are young? It is this: that being rich, we are so poor; that being mighty, we can yet have nothing; that seeing, breathing, smelling, tasting all around us the impossible wealth and glory of this earth, feeling with an intolerable certitude that the whole structure of the enchanted life—the most fortunate, wealthy, good, and happy life that any man has ever known—

is ours—is ours at once, immediately and forever, the moment that we choose to take a step, or stretch a hand, or say a word—we yet know that we can really keep, hold, take, and possess forever—nothing. All passes; nothing lasts: the moment that we put our hand upon it, it melts away like smoke, and is gone forever, and the snake is eating at our heart again; we see then what we are and what our lives must come to.

A young man is so strong, so mad, so certain, and so lost. He has everything and he is able to use nothing. He hurls the great shoulder of his strength forever against phantasmal barriers, he is a wave whose power explodes in lost mid-oceans under timeless skies, he reaches out to grip a fume of painted smoke, he wants all, feels the thirst and power for everything, and finally gets nothing. In the end, he is destroyed by his own strength, devoured by his own hunger, impoverished by his own wealth. Thoughtless of money or the accumulation of material possessions, he is none the less defeated in the end by his own greed a greed that makes the avarice of King Midas seem paltry by comparison.

And that is the reason why, when

youth is gone, every man will look back upon that period of his life with infinite sorrow and regret. It is the bitter sorrow and regret of a man who knows that once he had a great talent and wasted it, of a man who knows that once he had a great treasure and got nothing from it, of a man who knows that he had strength enough for everything and never used it.

不要为成功而努力，要为做一个有价值的人而努力。

——爱因斯坦

　　青春奇妙无穷，充满魅力，充满痛楚。青春年少的时候根本不知青春为何物，直到青春一去不复返了才对青春有了真正的认识。谁都想让青春永驻，不忍青春离去；眼睁睁地看着青春流逝，心中会涌起无穷的忧伤和惋惜；青春的失去是人们永远感到悲哀的事；青春的失去是人们真正觉得悲喜交集的事；即便奇迹出现青春复苏，谁都不会心甘情愿重度青春的岁月。

　　为什么如此？因为在青春时代，生活充满了奇特而辛酸的不可思议的事。我们在青春年少时带着悲喜交集的心情，十分强烈而不可名状地感受到人生的奇特辛酸、不可思议的经历。其实质是什么呢？

其实质是这样的：青春年少的时候，虽然殷实富足，却非常贫穷；虽然力气强大，却一无所有；世间的富贵荣华触目皆是，简直可以呼吸到，闻到嗅到，还可以品尝到，心中的自信按捺不住，深切地感受到整个被陶醉了的生活——人类迄今为止所知道的最幸运、最富有的美好幸福的生活，只要我们决定向前迈步，奋发努力，便立即归我们所有了，并将永远属于我们。然而，我们知道，我们真的永远不能抓到什么，永远不能获得什么，永远不能占有什么。一切匆匆过去，荡然无存。我们一出手它就烟消云散，飘然而去，一去不复返了。于是，心中泛起阵阵隐痛，看到了自己真实的面孔，看到了自己未来生活的必然走向。

青年人非常坚强，狂热自信，但容易迷惘混沌，虽然机缘无数，却把握不住，虽然身强体壮，试图冲破重重虚幻的屏障，却如同一个波浪，最终还是无力地消失在旷远浩渺的大海中央，他伸出手想要抓住斑斓的云烟，他想得到世间的万物，渴望主宰一切，最终却是一无所获。最后，他被自己的力量所毁灭，被自己的饥饿所吞食，被自己的财富弄得贫穷潦倒。他对金钱或财富的积累不以为然，然而最终还是被自己的贪欲所吞噬。

青春消逝，蓦然回首，无论是谁，心中都会充满无尽的忧伤，

充满无穷的懊悔。曾经才智卓越，却白白浪费了；曾经财富殷实，

却一无所有；曾经本事高强，却从未利用。一个认识到自己失落青

春的人回忆起来总是充满悲伤和懊悔。

词汇识记

wonderful ['wʌndəful] *adj.* 精彩的，极好的；惊人的，奇妙的

例：The vase made by the artisan is wonderful.

那个手艺人做的花瓶棒极了。

infinite ['ɪnfɪnət] *adj.* 无限的，无穷的，无边无际的

例：The number of positive numbers is infinite.

正数的数目是无穷的。

intolerable [ɪn'tɒlərəbl] *adj.* 无法忍受的，难耐的

例：There is intolerable noise outdoors.

门外是难以忍受的嘈杂声。

destroy [dɪ'strɔɪ] *v.* 破坏，毁灭

例：The whole edifice of his hopes was destroyed.

他心中的希望整个都毁了。

regret [rɪ'gret] *n.* 懊悔，遗憾，抱歉

例：We informed her with regret of our decision.

我们遗憾地把我们的决定通知她。

The moment that we choose to take a step, or stretch a hand....

choose to: 愿意（选定）

造句: _____

In the end, he is destroyed by his own strength, devoured by his own hunger, impoverished by his own wealth.

in the end: 最后，结果

造句: _____

青春奇妙无穷，充满魅力，充满痛楚。

译: _____

然而，我们知道，我们真的永远不能抓到什么，永远不能获得什么，永远不能占有什么。

译: _____

A Lesson for Living
生活给我上的一课

If you would go up high, then use your own legs! Do not let yourselves carried aloft; do not seat yourselves on other people's backs and heads.

—F. W . Nietzsche

"Everything happens for the best," my mother said whenever I faced disappointment. "If you carry on, one day something good will happen. And you'll realize that it wouldn't have happened if not for that previous disappointment."

Mother was right, as I discovered after graduating from college in 1932. I had decided to try for a job in radio, then work my way up to sports announcer. I hitchhiked to Chicago and knocked on the door of every station—and got turned down every time.

In one studio, a kind lady told me that big stations couldn't risk hiring an inexperienced person. "Go out in the sticks and find a small station that'll give you a chance," she said.

I thumbed home to Dixon, Illinois. While there was no radio-announcing jobs in Dixon, my father said Montgomery Ward had opened a store and wanted a local athlete to manage its sports department. Since Dixon was where I had played high school football, I applied. The job sounded just right for me. But I wasn't hired.

My disappointment must have shown. "Everything happens for the best," Mom reminded me. Dad offered me the car to job-hunting. I tried WOC Radio in Davenport, Iowa. The program director, a wonderful Scotsman named Peter MacArthur, told me they had already hired an announcer.

As I left his office, my frustration boiled over. I asked aloud, "How can a fellow get to be a sports announcer if he can't get a job in a radio station?"

I was waiting for the elevator when I heard MacArthur calling, "What was that you said about sports? Do you know anything about football?" Then he stood me before a microphone and asked me to broadcast an imaginary game.

On my way home, as I have many times since, I thought of my mother's words: "If you carry on, one day something good will happen. Something wouldn't have happened if not for that previous disappointment."

I often wonder what direction my life might have taken if I'd gotten the job at Montgomery Ward.

如果你想走到高处，就要使用自己的两条腿！不要让别人把你抬到
高处；不要坐在别人的背上和头上。

——弗里德里希·威廉·尼采

　　每当我遇到挫折时，母亲就会说："一切都会好的。如果你坚持
下去，总有一天会有好事发生。你会认识到，如果没有以前的挫折，
就不会有现在的一切。"

　　母亲是对的，发现这一点是在1932年，我刚从大学毕业。我已
决定试着在电台找个事儿做，然后争取做体育节目的播音员。我搭便
车到了芝加哥，挨家电台地敲门推销自己——但每次都被拒绝了。

　　在一个播音室里，一位好心的女士告诉我，大的广播电台是不会
冒险雇佣没经验的新手的。"去乡下找一家给你机会的小电台吧。"
她说。

　　我搭车回到我的家乡，那是伊利诺伊州的迪克森。在迪克森当时
还没有电台播音员这样的工作，父亲说，蒙哥马利·沃德开了一家新
商店，想雇一个本地的运动员管理店里的体育部。我中学时曾在迪克
森打过橄榄球，出于这个原因我去申请了这份工作。工作听起来挺适
合我的，但是我没被聘用。

我的沮丧心情一定表现出来了。"一切总会好的。"母亲提醒我。爸爸给我买了一辆汽车以便于找工作用。我试着到爱荷华州达文波特的WOC电台去求职。那里的电台节目负责人是一个很棒的苏格兰人，名叫彼得·麦克阿瑟，他告诉我他们已经雇到播音员了。

　　离开他办公室时，我愤怒极了。我大声地说："一个连在电台都找不到工作的家伙又怎么能成为体育节目的播音员呢？"

　　等电梯时，我听见麦克阿瑟喊道："你说什么体育？你了解橄榄球吗？"接着，他让我站到麦克风前，请我解说一场想象中的比赛。

　　在回家的路上——以后也有很多次地，我思考着母亲的那些话："如果你坚持下去，总有一天会有好事发生。如果没有以前的挫折，就不会有现在的一切。"

　　我常想，如果我当年得到了蒙哥马利·沃德的那份工作，我的人生之路又会怎样走呢？

词汇识记

disappointment [ˌdɪsəˈpɔɪntmənt] *n.* 挫折

例：After months of disappointment, his perseverance was finally rewarded.

数月来他经历挫折而不断努力，终于有了收获。

risk [rɪsk] *v.* 冒险

例：He saved my life at the risk of his own.

他冒着自己的生命危险救了我的命。

frustration [frʌ'streɪʃən] *n.* 挫折，阻挠

例：Finally, in frustration, he just blew his stack.

最后在灰心丧气的情况下，他就大发雷霆了。

短语搭配

I had decided to try for a job in radio, then work my way up to sports announcer.

work one's way up: 通过努力一步步地升上去

造句：＿＿＿＿＿＿＿＿＿＿＿＿＿＿＿＿＿＿＿＿＿

I hitchhiked to Chicago and knocked on the door of every station—and got turned down every time.

knock on: 敲（门、窗等）

造句：＿＿＿＿＿＿＿＿＿＿＿＿＿＿＿＿＿＿＿＿＿

I was waiting for the elevator when I heard MacArthur calling…

wait for: 等候，等待

造句：＿＿＿＿＿＿＿＿＿＿＿＿＿＿＿＿＿＿＿＿＿

译展身手

如果你坚持下去，总有一天会有好事发生。

译：＿＿＿＿＿＿＿＿＿＿＿＿＿＿＿＿＿＿＿＿＿

你会认识到，如果没有以前的挫折就不会有现在的一切。

译：＿＿＿＿＿＿＿＿＿＿＿＿＿＿＿＿＿＿＿＿＿

A New Look from Borrowed Time
第二次生命的启示

We can't all be heroes. Somebody has to sit on the curb and clap as they go by.

—W. Roger

Just ten years ago I sat across the desk from a doctor with a stethoscope. "Yes," he said, "there is a lesion in the left upper lobe. You have a moderately advanced case…" I listened, stunned, as he continued: "You'll have to give up work at once and go to bed. Later on, we'll see … " He gave me no assurance.

Feeling like a man who in mid-career has suddenly been placed under sentence of death with an indefinite reprieve, I left the doctor's office, walked over to the park and sat down on a bench—perhaps, as I then told myself, for the last time. I needed to think.

In the next three days I cleared up my affairs. Then I went home, got into bed and set my watch to tick off not the minutes but the months.

Two and a half years, and many dashed hopes later, I left my bed and began the long climb back. It was another year before I made it.

I speak of this experience because these years that passes so slowly taught me what to value and what to believe. They said to me: Take time before time takes you.

I realize now that this world I'm living in is not my oyster to be opened, but my opportunity to be grasped. Each day to rile is a precious entity. The sun comes up and presents me with twenty-four brand new, wonderful hours—not to pass but to fill. I've learned to appreciate those little all important things I never thought I had the time to notice before the play of light on running water, the music of the wind in my favorite pine tree.

I seem now to see and hear and feel with some of the recovered freshness of childhood. How well, for instance, I recall the touch of the spring earth under my feet the day I first stepped upon it after the years in bed. It was almost more than I could bear. It was like regaining one's citizenship in a world one had nearly lost.

Frequently I sit back and say to myself: Let me make note of this moment I'm living right now. Because in it I'm well, happy, hard at work doing what I like best to do. It won't always be like this; so while it is, I'll make the most of it. And afterwards, I'll remember and be grateful.

All this I owe to that long time spent "on the sidelines" of life. Wiser people come to this awareness without having to acquire it the hard way. But I wasn't wise enough. I'm wiser now a little and happier.

"Look thy last on all things lovely every hour!"With these words Walter de la Mare sums up for me my philosophy and my belief. God made this world in spite of what man now and then tries to do to unmake it a dwelling place of beauty and wonder, and He filled it with more goodness than most of us suspect. And so I say to myself. Should I not pretty often take time to absorb the beauty and the wonder... to contribute at least a little to the goodness? And should I not then, in my heart, give thanks? Truly I do. This I believe.

我们不可能都成为英雄。总得有人在英雄走过的时候坐在路边鼓掌。

——罗杰

　　就在10年前，我与拿着听诊器的医生相对而坐。他说："你的左肺叶上部有一处坏损，病情正在恶化……"听到这些，我顿时愣住了，他接着说道："你必须放下工作，卧床休息。稍后，我们会对你进行进一步的观察……"对于我的病情，医生也不是太确定。

　　事业正如日中天的我突然感觉像被判了刑，而刑期却尚未确定。我走出医生的办公室，坐在公园的长椅上，自言自语道，这也许是最后一次了。我需要好好想一想。

　　接下来的3天里，我处理完手上所有的事务，然后，回到家，躺在床上，将手表的显示从分钟改为月份。

　　之后两年半的时间里，我经历了无数次失望的打击，最终离开病榻，开始缓慢地恢复原来的生活状态。第二年，我成功了。

　　提及这段经历，是因为过去这段漫长的岁月让我懂得了什么值得珍惜，什么值得信仰。它们告诉我：好好把握时间，而不要让时间支配你。

如今我意识到，我所生存的这个世界并不是等待我去打开的贝壳，而是等待我去把握的机遇。对我而言，每一天都是稀世珍宝。太阳每次升起，都会带给我崭新而精彩的24小时——我绝不能虚度。我学会了去欣赏生活细节的美好，比如水面的粼粼波光，松间风儿的轻吟——这些重要的生活细节我从前竟无暇理会。

如今，我的所见、所闻、所感总会带给我一种清新的感觉，让我仿佛回到了童年。当我离开多年的病榻，双脚再次踏上大地时，那松软的土壤带给我的美好感觉令我激动不已。那种感觉就像重新获得了差点失之交臂的世界。

我常常会惬意地坐着，告诉自己：要珍惜现在的每一分每一秒。因为此刻的我健康、快乐，并在为自己最喜爱的工作而努力奋斗。然而这些美好终会消逝；因此，我要加倍珍惜这存在的每一刻。等它消逝后，我会记住这些美好，并心存感激。

在生命边缘徘徊的那些漫长岁月，让我明白了这一切。而智者不必经历这样的艰难也能意识到这些，从前的我实在是愚钝。如今，我多了几分聪慧，也多了几分快乐。

"时刻铭记，最后再看一眼那些可爱的事物！"英国诗人沃尔特·德拉·梅尔的这句话正好阐述了我人生的哲学与信仰。尽管人类现在总试图毁灭这个世界，但上帝创造了它，创造了这个美丽而奇妙的家园，并赋予了它超乎我们想象的美好。因此，我告诉自己：这些美丽与精彩难道不值得我去细细体味……我不应为世间的美好奉献出自己微薄的力量吗？难道我不应心存感激？的确，我相信，我应该这么做。

词汇识记

assurance [ə'ʃuə:rəns] *n.* 把握，信心；保证；(人寿)保险

例：They were waiting with assurance for me to discover the truth for myself.

他们自信地等待我自己发现事实真相。

appreciate [ə'pri:ʃieɪt] *v.* 欣赏，赏识；感激；领会，意识到

例：We appreciate your helping us.

我们感谢你们的帮助。

citizenship ['sɪtɪzənʃɪp] *n.* 公（市）民身份；国籍

例：She was German by birth but is now of French citizenship.

她在德国出生但现在是法国国籍。

dwelling ['dwelɪŋ] *n.* 住处

例：Behind every apartment-houses, beside each dwelling were small garages.

每一座公寓房子后面和每一所住房旁边都有小小的汽车房。

短语搭配

Then I went home, got into bed and set my watch to tick off not the minutes but the months.

tick off: 给……标，用记号勾出；责备；激怒

造句：_____

Let me make note of this moment I'm living right now.

make note of: 打草稿；做笔记

造句：＿＿＿＿＿＿＿＿＿＿＿＿＿＿＿＿＿＿＿＿＿＿＿＿＿＿＿＿

译展身手

提及这段经历，是因为过去这段漫长的岁月让我懂得了什么值得珍惜，
什么值得信仰。

译：＿＿＿＿＿＿＿＿＿＿＿＿＿＿＿＿＿＿＿＿＿＿＿＿＿＿＿＿

对我而言，每一天都是稀世珍宝。

译：＿＿＿＿＿＿＿＿＿＿＿＿＿＿＿＿＿＿＿＿＿＿＿＿＿＿＿＿

但上帝创造了它，创造了这个美丽而奇妙的家园，并赋予了它超乎我们
想象的美好。

译：＿＿＿＿＿＿＿＿＿＿＿＿＿＿＿＿＿＿＿＿＿＿＿＿＿＿＿＿

Four Seasons of a Tree
树的四季

In delay there lies no plenty, then come kiss me, sweet and twenty, Youth's a stuff that will not endure.

—William Shakespeare

There was a man. He had four sons. He wanted his sons to learn not to judge things to go and look at a pear tree that was far away.

The first son went in the winter, the second in the spring, the third in summer, the youngest son in fall. When they had all gone and come back, he called them together to describe what they had seen.

The first son said that the tree was ugly, bent and weak.

The second son said no—it was covered with green buds and full of promise.

The third son said it was laden with blossoms and they smelt so sweet and looked so beautiful.

The last son disagreed with all of them. He said it was ripe and droop with fruit, full of life and fulfilment.

The man then said to his sons that they were all right, because they each had seen but only one season in the tree's life.

He told them that they cannot judge a tree or a person, by only one season, and that the essence of who they are—the pleasure, the joy and love that come from that life—can only be measured at the end, when all the seasons are up.

If you give up when it is winter, you will miss the promise of your spring, the beauty of your summer, the fulfilment of your fall. Don't let the pain of one season destroy the joy of all the rest.

迁延蹉跎，来日无多，二十丽姝，请来吻我，衰草枯杨，青春易过。

——威廉·莎士比亚

从前，一个父亲有四个儿子。他希望儿子们能学会凡事勿匆匆下结论，于是轮番派遣他们到很远的地方去观察一棵梨树。

大儿子是冬天去的，二儿子春天启程，老三去时已是炎热的夏季，老四于金秋时节踏上了征程。待他们全都观树归来以后，父亲把他们叫到一起，听他们各自描述自己的所见。

大儿子数落说大树枝弯干斜，很难看。

二儿子连忙否认，说树上发满嫩绿的新芽，生机盎然。

老三不同意了，树上明明开满鲜花，吐露芬芳，漂亮极了。

他们的说法实在让老四哑然，枝头上坠满的难道不是累累果实，在彰显生机与收获吗？

　　父亲解释说，儿子们的说法都没错，因为他们看到的是大树一年四个季节里的不同情景。

　　他告诉儿子们说，不能以一季来判断树，更不能以一时来判断人，因为人之本质——源自他们喜、乐、爱的根本——只有在其生之了结时，才可盖棺论定。

　　倘若你在冬季就已放弃，那无疑会错过春季的生机、夏季的美丽和秋季的收益。勿为一季的痛苦而破坏了所有的欢乐。

词汇识记

judge [dʒʌdʒ] *v.* 断定，判断；裁决，评定；审判

例：I judge him to be about 40.

我断定他有40来岁。

describe [dɪ'skraɪb] *v.* 描述，形容

例：The police asked me to describe exactly how it happened.

警察让我描述一下这事是怎样发生的。

ugly ['ʌɡlɪ] *adj.* 难看的，丑（陋）的；可怕的，恐怖的

例：Toads have an ugly appearance but they are useful.

蟾蜍外表丑陋，但很有用。

essence ['esns] *n.* 本质，实质，要素；精髓，精华

例：Simplicity is the essence of good taste.

纯朴是情趣高尚的主要因素。

短语搭配

The second son said no—it was covered with green buds and full of promise.

be covered with: 有大量的（满是，被……覆盖）

造句: ＿＿＿＿＿＿＿＿＿＿＿＿＿＿＿＿＿＿＿＿＿＿＿

The last son disagreed with all of them. He said it was ripe and droop with fruit…

disagree with: 不同意

造句: ＿＿＿＿＿＿＿＿＿＿＿＿＿＿＿＿＿＿＿＿＿＿＿

译展身手

不能以一季来判断树，更不能以一时来判断人。

译: ＿＿＿＿＿＿＿＿＿＿＿＿＿＿＿＿＿＿＿＿＿＿＿

倘若你在冬季就已放弃，那无疑会错过春季的生机、夏季的美丽和秋季的收益。

译: ＿＿＿＿＿＿＿＿＿＿＿＿＿＿＿＿＿＿＿＿＿＿＿

Life Lessons I've Learned
关于人生的课程

The most glorious moment in your life are not the so-called days of success, but rather those days when out of dejection and despair you feel rise in you a challenge to life, and the promise of future accomplishment.

—Gustave Flaubert

At the age of 7: One can't hide a piece of broccoli in a glass of milk.

I like my teacher because she cries when we sing *Silent Night*.

9: When I wave to people in the country, they stop what they are doing and wave back.

13: Just when I get my room the way I like it, Mom makes me clean it up.

If you want to cheer yourself up, you should try cheering someone else up first.

15: Although it's hard to admit it, I'm secretly glad that my parents are strict with me.

24: Silent company is often more healing than words of advice.

29: Brushing my child's hair is one of life's great pleasures.

Wherever I go, the world's worst drivers have followed me there.

39: If someone says something unkind about me, I must live so that no one will believe it.

41: There are people who love you dearly but just don't know how to show it.

44: You can make someone's day by simply sending him / her a small card.

46: Children and grandparents are natural allies.

The greater a person's sense of guilt, the greater his / her need to cast blame on others.

50: Motel mattresses are better on the side away from the phone.

52: You can tell a lot about a man by the way he handles these three things: a rainy day, lost luggage, and tangled Christmas tree lights.

53: Regardless of your relationship with your parents, you miss them terribly after they die.

61: If you want to do something positive for your children, try to improve your marriage.

62: Life sometimes gives you a second chance.

64: You shouldn't go through life with a catcher's mitt on both hands. You need to be able to throw something back.

65: If you pursue happiness, it will elude you. But if you focus on your family, the needs of others, your work, meeting new people, and doing the very best you can, happiness will find you.

66: Whenever I decide something with kindness, I usually make the right decision.

73: It pays to believe in miracles. And to tell the truth, I've seen several.

82: Even when I have pains, I don't have to be one.

85: Making a living is not the same as making a life. Every day you should reach out and touch someone. People love that human touch, holding hands, a warm hug, or just a friendly pat on the back.

92: I still have a lot to learn.

人的一生中，最为辉煌的时刻并不是功成名就的那些天，而是从悲叹与绝望中产生对人生的挑战和对未来辉煌的期盼的那些日子。

——古斯塔夫·福楼拜

7岁时：不能把一片花椰菜藏在一杯牛奶里面。

我喜欢我的老师，因为我们一起唱《平安夜》时她会哭。

9岁时：当我向乡下的人们挥手时，他们会停下手中的活，向我挥手。

13岁时：当我把自己的房间摆设成自己喜欢的样子时，妈妈让我把它收拾干净。

如果想让自己高兴，就应该先试着让别人高兴。

15岁时：尽管不愿承认，但私底下我很高兴父母对我严加管教。

24岁时：默默地陪伴常常比建议性的话语更能治疗(别人的)创伤。

29岁时：给我的孩子梳头是人生一大乐事。

无论走到哪里，我都会碰到最差的司机。

39岁时：如果有人说我的坏话，我必须活下去，那样就没人会相信那些话了。

41岁时：有的人非常爱你，但就是不知道如何表现出来。

44岁时：仅仅送某人一张小贺卡，你就可以让他（她）很高兴。

46岁时：孩子和祖父母常常一拍即合。

一个人的罪恶感越强，他（她）嫁祸于他人的需求就越大。

50岁时：汽车旅馆的床垫在远离电话的那一边更好。

52岁时：看一个男人如何应对下雨天、丢失的行李和圣诞树上缠绕在一起的灯，你就可以看出他是怎样一个人。

53岁时：不管你和父母的关系如何，一旦他们去世了，你对他们的思念会非常强烈。

61岁时：如果你想为你的孩子做些积极的事，那就设法改善你的婚姻。

62岁时：有时候，生活会给你第二次机会。

64岁时：你不应该一辈子双手都戴着接球员的手套，你必须能够扔回某些东西。

65岁时：如果你去追赶幸福，幸福就会躲着你，但如果你把精力集中在家庭、他人的需求、你的工作、认识新的人和尽最大努力做事，幸福就会找上门。

66岁时：无论何时，善意的决定通常都是正确的决定。

73岁时：相信奇迹的出现是有代价的。老实说，我已经看见过好几个奇迹了。

82岁时：感到痛苦的时候，也不要成为(别人的)痛苦。

85岁时：谋生不等同于生活。每天你都应该伸出手去碰触别人。人们喜欢这种人性的接触、牵手、温暖的拥抱或仅仅友好地拍拍后背。

92岁时：我要学的东西还有很多。

词汇识记

admit [əd'mɪt] v. 承认，允许进入
例：I must admit, it's more difficult than I thought it would be.
我必须承认，这比我想象的要困难得多。

pleasure ['pleʒə(r)] n. 愉快，高兴，快事
例：He listened with pleasure to the beautiful music.
他陶醉在美妙的音乐中。

blame [bleɪm] *n.* 责备，过失

例：We were ready to take the blame for what had happened.

我们准备对所发生的事承担责任。

handle ['hændl] *v.* 处理，对待

例：An officer must know how to handle his men.

当军官的应懂得怎样统率士兵。

短语搭配

Just when I get my room the way I like it, Mom makes me clean it up.

clean up:（把……）收拾干净；清理，清除

造句：_____

Although it's hard to admit it, I'm secretly glad that my parents are strict with me.

be strict with: 对……要求严格

造句：_____

Regardless of your relationship with your parents, you miss them terribly after they die.

regardless of: 不管，不顾

造句：_____

译展身手

有的人非常爱你，但就是不知道如何表现出来。

译：_____

无论何时，善意的决定通常都是正确的决定。

译：_____

Never Give Up Your Dreams
永远别放弃梦想

Do not, for one repulse, give Up the purpose that you resolved to effect.
—William Shakespeare

The first day of school our professor introduced himself and challenged us to get to know someone we didn't already know. I stood up to look around when a gentle hand touched my shoulder. I turned around to find a wrinkled, little old lady beaming up at me with a smile that lit up her entire being. She said, "Hi handsome. My name is Rose. I'm eighty-seven years old. Can I give you a hug?"I laughed and enthusiastically responded, "Of course you may. "And she gave me a giant squeeze.

"Why are you in college at such a young, innocent age?" I asked. She jokingly replied, "I'm here to meet a rich husband, get married, have a couple of children, and then retire and travel. ""No, seriously?"I asked. I was curious what may have motivated her to be taking on this challenge at her age.

"I always dreamed of having a college education and now I'm getting one."she told me. After class we walked to the student union building and shared a chocolate milk shake. We became instant friends.

Every day for the next three months we would leave class together and talk nonstop. I was always mesmerized listening to this "time machine" as she shared her wisdom and experience with me.

Over the course of the year, Rose became a campus icon and she easily made friends wherever she went. She loved to dress up and she reveled in the attention bestowed up her from the other students. She was living it up. At the end of the semester we invited Rose to speak at our football banquet. I'll never forget what she taught us. She was introduced and stepped up to the podium. As she began to deliver her prepared speech, she dropped her three by five cards on the floor. Frustrated and a little embarrassed she leaned into the microphone and simply said, "I'm sorry I'm so jittery. I gave up beer for Lent and this whisky is killing me. I'll never get my speech back in order so let me just tell you what I know. "As we laughed she cleared her throat and began: "We do not stop playing because we are old; we grow old because we stop playing. There are only four secrets to staying young, being happy, and achieving success."

"You have to laugh and find humor every day."

"You've got to have a dream. When you lose your dreams, you die. We have so many people walking around who are dead and don't even know it."

"There is a huge difference between growing older and growing up. If you are nineteen years old and lie in bed for one full year and don't do one productive thing, you will turn twenty years old. If I am eighty-seven years old and stay in bed for a year and never do anything I will turn eighty-eight. Anybody can grow older. That doesn't take any talent or ability. The idea is to grow up by always finding the opportunity in change."

"Have no regrets. The elderly usually don't have regrets for what we did, but rather for things we did not do. The only people who fear death are those with regrets."

She concluded her speech by courageously singing "The Rose." She challenged each of us to study the lyrics and live them out in our daily lives.

At the year's end Rose finished the college degree she had begun all those years ago. One week after graduation Rose died peacefully in her sleep.

Over two thousand college students attended her funeral in tribute to the wonderful woman who taught by example that it's never too late to be all you can possibly be.

Remember, growing older is mandatory, growing up is optional.

不要只因一次失败，就放弃你原来决心要达到的目的。

——威廉·莎士比亚

开学的第一天教授做了自我介绍，他还要求我们去结识某位我们还不认识的人。就在我站起来四处张望时，一只手轻轻地搭在了我的肩上。我转过身一看，一位满脸皱纹个子矮小的老太太正冲着我微笑。这微笑使她浑身光彩照人。她说："嘿，帅小伙儿，我叫罗斯，今年87岁。我可以拥抱你吗？"我笑了起来，热情地答道："当然可以啦。"她紧紧地拥抱了我。

"你为什么在这么年轻而天真的年龄上大学？"我问。她开玩笑地回答说："我要在此遇到一个有钱的丈夫，结婚，生几个孩子，然后退休，去旅游。""真的吗？不对吧？"我问她。我很想知道，她这么大年纪，是什么促使她接受这样的挑战。

"我一直梦想接受大学教育。而现在我如愿以偿了。"她告诉我说。课后我们一同到学生活动楼，共饮了一杯巧克力泡沫牛奶。我们一下子就成了朋友。在此后的三个月中，我们每天都一起离开课堂，聊起来没完没了。在她向我传授她的智慧和经验时，我总是着了迷似的倾听这个"时间机器"。

在这一年里，罗斯成了校园里的偶像。不管到哪里，她很容易地就交上了朋友。她喜欢精心打扮，陶醉于其他学生对她的注意。她尽情地享受这一切。到学期末，我们请罗斯在我们的足球宴会上讲话。我永远也不会忘记她给我们的教诲。介绍完毕后她就登上讲台。正当她要开始已准备好的演讲时，她的5寸长3寸宽的卡片掉在了地上。她有些不知所措，还有点尴尬，于是就靠近话筒干脆说了起来："很抱歉我这么紧张。我为大斋节戒了啤酒，而这威士忌可是毁了我。按原先准备好了的讲是不可能了，还是把我所知道的说给你们听吧。"我们都笑了，她则清了清嗓子开始说："我们并不因为自己老了而不娱乐；我们因为停止了娱乐而变老。要想保持年轻，过得幸福并取得成功只有4条秘诀。"

"每天都要笑，每天都要找到幽默。"

"一定要有梦想。失去了梦想，人就死了。在我们周围有那么多行尸走肉般的人，他们却不自知。"

"变老和成熟是有巨大区别的。如果你19岁，在床上躺一整年，而不做一件有成效的事情，你会到20岁。如果我87岁，在床上待一年什么也不做，我也会到88岁。谁都会老，那不需要天才或能力。我的意思是要通过在变化中不断地寻找机会而达到成熟。"

"不要后悔。年长的人一般不会为我们所做的事而后悔，而会为我们所没有做的事后悔。只有充满遗憾的人才惧怕死亡。"

她勇敢地唱了一首《玫瑰之歌》作为结束，还要求我们每个人学习歌词并在日常生活中将词意付诸行动。

年末，罗斯结束了她多年前就开始的大学生涯，取得了学位。毕业一周之后，罗斯在睡梦中平静地去世。

两千多名大学生出席了她的葬礼，对这位了不起的女士表示敬意。她以自身范例教育我们：发挥自己的潜能永不为晚。

记住，衰老是无法抗拒的，而成熟却是可以选择的。

词汇识记

squeeze [skwi:z] *n.* 挤；榨取；挤过

例：We managed to get all the luggage into the car but it was a tight squeeze.

我们总算把行李都塞进汽车里了，不过挤得要命。

motivate ['məʊtɪveɪt] *v.* 作为……的动机，激励，激发

例：He may be motivated to produce more in the future.

那就会促使他以后生产更多的商品。

mandatory ['mændətəri] *adj.* 强制性的

例：It's mandatory to pay taxes.

缴税是义务性的。

短语搭配

I turned around to find a wrinkled, little old lady beaming up at me with a smile that lit up her entire being.

turn around: 转身

造句：_____

She loved to dress up and she reveled in the attention bestowed up her from the other students.

dress up: 穿上盛装，精心打扮；装饰，修饰

造句：_____

译展身手

记住，衰老是无法抗拒的，而成熟却是可以选择的。

译：_____

每天都要笑，每天都要找到幽默。

译：_____

The Gift of Life
生命的礼物

There is only one success—to be able to spend your life in your own way.

—C. Morley

I am not someone who had ever given back to the community. My father had drilled into my sisters and me all our lives that charity begins at home, and so I gave generously to family and friends, but rarely to any cause outside of that. I have always greatly admired those who volunteer their time and money and are in the trenches helping other human beings when they are in the most need. I have a side of me that is very compassionate, and my heart breaks when I watch news reports of the Red Cross helping storm victims after hurricanes or tornadoes that destroyed everything but the clothes on their backs. Only I have never been compelled to do anything to help the effort, not even to write out a check.

I always felt bad about that, but even guilt didn't motivate me to do anything about it. I preferred not to think about all the suffering in the world, and I did this by switching the station on the TV whenever a "Feed the Children" commercial came on. Out of sight, out of mind was how I dealt with all the suffering in the world.

In my mind, I often defended myself, saying I was just so sensitive to other people suffering, and that I would only suffer myself if I got too close and personal to it. I knew I could never be in the trenches with people when they were in dire needs, because I'd probably be as upset and emotional as they were. I told myself that's not what they needed, for me to feel sorry for them and cry with them. What they needed was comfort, yes, but most importantly they needed someone to give them hope, and I never trusted that I could give that to anyone.

Several months ago, my 22-year-old niece phoned me. "Aunt Lene," she said in her sweet voice that never fails to melt my heart, " the blood bank called and asked if I would donate blood. Would you come and donate with me?" I couldn't refuse her.

The first and only time I had donated blood was during the Gulf War ten years ago. My best friend was a nurse in a M. A. S. H. unit on the front line, and I did it for her. I also sent her a care package full of goodies and necessities she couldn't get over there in the middle of hell. I remember how good it made me feel to do this for her.

I didn't know before going to the blood bank, that I would be able to donate blood in the name of someone specific. There was a bulletin board with photos of children who were patients at Children's Hospital. It was the same hospital where I had lost my daughter to cancer two years prior, so my heart went out to these children who were battling life threatening illnesses. One photo was of a little black girl, only 9 years old, and her beautiful face, although swollen from drugs, spoke to me. Her name was Alexis, and she was battling cancer. She had been fighting the disease most of her life, and I read where she had been in remission twice, but the cancer had returned for a third time. I requested to donate my blood in Alexis's name.

I braved the needle and the procedure was relatively painless, The blood bank wanted to give me a stuffed animal and a T-shirt, but I declined. I wasn't there to get anything for my effort, but was there only to give. A month and a half later, I went back, and then a month and a half after that, I went back again. I felt this was something I could do, and so I made a promise to myself to go as often as I could while I was in good health.

I hardly watch TV, but I do keep the TV on in the morning while I'm getting ready for work. Although I am not in front of the TV, I am listening to it. One morning I heard a news broadcaster reporting about a young girl named Alexis, and I immediately went to the TV to see if he was talking about my Alexis from the blood bank. She was.

Alexis had lost her battle with cancer, and my heart broke. As I sat with tears running down my face. I listened to Alexis's story, and the legacy she left behind. I wasn't surprised to hear what an extraordinary child Alexis was because I saw it in her eyes when I saw her photograph at the blood bank. She had the most angelic face, and a smile that was so full of joy and courage, that she endeared herself to me instantly.

It was no coincidence that I learned of Alexis's life and death that morning. She was an angel now, and she saw the big picture, and knew it was important for me to know that what I was doing by giving blood may not seem like a big thing to me, but it was to her, and it is to all the children who are still fighting the fight like she did.

I never met this wonderful child, never touched her, but she surely touched me. Her spirit went right to my soft spot, and I will never forget her. I like to think she is a great friend to my daughter on the other side, and they are happy, healthy, laughing and playing like little girls should.

My therapist is always telling me that even though I do something that doesn't take much of my time, effort or money, it doesn't mean that what I do has no value. Every little thing we do to help another has value to the one who needs it, so I encourage you all to do what you can. A dollar here, a dollar there, a minute here, a minute there, a gesture here, a gesture there will all add up.

只有一种成功，那就是能够用自己的方式度过自己的一生。

——莫利

我没有回报过社会。父亲时常教导我和姐姐，仁爱始于家庭。因而，我慷慨地给予家人和朋友关爱，但没为别人做过什么。我一直很钦佩那些人——他们自愿花时间和金钱救助身处困境的人们。当然，我也富有同情心，当看到报道红十字会拯救遭飓风袭击的灾民时，我的心都碎了，要知道，除了身上的衣服，这些难民失去了一切。我从来没有援助过任何人，也从未捐过款。

我常因此感到不安，即便如此，这种负罪感也没能激发我做任何关爱他人的事。我宁愿不去想世间的苦难，所以，看电视时，只要有

"援助儿童"的广告，我就换频道。眼不见，心不烦——这就是我对待世间苦难的方式。

内心中，我常为自己找借口，比如我对他人疾苦过于敏感，倘若过分关注，自己也会深感痛苦。我很清楚，自己不可能救人于危难。卷入他们的生活，只会让自己像他们一样沮丧、心烦意乱。我告诉自己，那不是他们真正需要的，他们也不想得到别人的同情；他们真正需要的是安慰，对，是精神慰藉，最重要的是，他们需要别人给予希望。而我从不相信自己能给谁希望。

数月后，我22岁的侄女打电话给我，她的声音非常甜美，总让我内心深受触动，"姑姑，血库打电话问我献不献血。你可以陪我去吗？"我同意了。

我第一次，也是仅有的一次献血是在十年前的海湾战争时期。那时，我最好的朋友是流动陆军外科医院的护士，我是因她才献血的。我还寄给她一个装满糖果和日用品的包裹，这些都是她在前线不可能有的。我记得我还为此很开心。

去血库前，我不知道会以具体人的名义献血。那里有一个公告栏，上面都是儿童医院小患者们的照片。两年前，正是在这家医院，我身患癌症的女儿离开了人世。因此，我很同情这些与绝症抗争的孩子们。有一张照片是一个九岁的黑人小女孩，由于药物缘故，她的小脸有些肿胀，但那漂亮的脸蛋似乎会说话。她叫亚里克西斯，正与病魔做斗争。她生命的大部分几乎都在与癌症抗争，我了解到，她的病情曾两次好转，但现在又恶化了，这已经是第三次了。于是，我请求以她的名义献血。

我不晕针，整个献血过程无丝毫疼痛。血库要赠我一个毛茸茸的小动物和一件T恤，我婉言谢绝了。我献血并非有所图，仅仅只是想献血。一个半月后，我又来献血。再一个半月后，我第三次献血。我觉得这是我力所能及的，因此我暗自发誓，只要身体健康，就经常来献血。

我几乎不看电视，但我坚持在上班前打开电视。虽然并没坐在电视前收看，但我能听到播放的内容。一天早上，我听到播音员报道一个名为亚里克西斯的小女孩。我立即上前看，想知道报道的是不是我在血库认识的那个小女孩，的确是她。

亚里克西斯在抗击绝症的过程中死去了，我非常伤心。我听着亚里克西斯的故事，泪流满面。报道说她是一个非常出色的孩子，对这一点我并不感到惊讶，因为

在血库的那张照片上，我从她的眼睛里就看出来了。她有着天使般的面庞，微笑中满是乐观和勇气。我看她第一眼，就喜欢上了她。

那天早上，我得知她的故事和死讯并非巧合。她现在是一个天使了，她觉得让我知道这一切很重要；于我而言，我的献血行为没什么大不了的，但对她，对那些在生命边缘挣扎的孩子们，却是极了不起的。

我从未见过这个了不起的孩子，也没接触过她。然而，她却深深地打动了我，她的精神触动了我灵魂的最深处，令我无法忘怀。我喜欢把她当作我女儿的好朋友，在另外一个世界里，她们很快乐、很健康，像所有小女孩一样，她们嬉笑着，玩闹着。

我的医疗师总对我说，尽管我做的事不占用太多时间，不花费太多气力和金钱，但这并不意味着我所做的没有价值。对需要帮助的人们，我们做的每件小事都意义深刻。因此，我建议你们，勿以善小而不为。点点滴滴的善行加起来，价值就不菲了。

词汇识记

volunteer [ˌvɒlənˈtɪə(r)] v. 自愿（做；提供）
例：The soldier volunteered for guard duty.
那个战士自告奋勇去站岗。

prefer [prɪˈfɜː(r)] v. 宁愿
例：She had had many proposals (of marriage) but preferred to remain single.

许多人向她求过婚，但她愿过独身生活。

remission [rɪ'mɪʃn] *n.* 宽恕，赦免

例：Remission of sins is promised to those who repent.

悔罪者可得到赦免。

endear [ɪn'dɪə(r)] *v.* 使受喜爱

例：He managed to endear himself to everyone.

他设法让大家都喜欢他。

短语搭配

I was just so sensitive to other people suffering, and that I would only suffer myself if I got too close and personal to it.

be sensitive to: 对……敏感(易感受)

造句：＿＿＿＿＿＿＿＿＿＿＿＿＿＿＿＿＿＿

I like to think she is a great friend to my daughter on the other side...

on the other side: 另一方面

造句：＿＿＿＿＿＿＿＿＿＿＿＿＿＿＿＿＿＿

译展身手

我几乎不看电视，但我坚持在上班前打开电视。

译：＿＿＿＿＿＿＿＿＿＿＿＿＿＿＿＿＿＿

点点滴滴的善行加起来，价值就不菲了。

译：＿＿＿＿＿＿＿＿＿＿＿＿＿＿＿＿＿＿

The Teacher Miss Bee
蜜蜂老师

Wherever you are sincerely pleased, you are nourished.

—Emerson

It is normal to go to the butcher's for meat, and the grocery store for food. But when I spent the summer with my grandmother, she sent me down to the general store with a list. How could I hope to find anything on the packed, jumbled shelves around me?

I walked up to the counter. Behind it was a lady like no one I'd ever seen.

"Excuse me," I said. She looked up.

"You're that Clements kid," she said. "I'm Miss Bee. Come closer and let me get a look at you." She pushed her glasses up her nose. "I want to be able to describe you to the sheriff if something goes missing from the store."

"I'm not a thief!" I was shocked. I was seven years, too young to be a thief!

"From what I can see you're not much of anything. But I can tell you've got potential."

"I need to get these," I said, holding up my list.

"So? Go get them. " Miss Bee pointed to a sign on the screen door. "There's no one here except you and me and I'm not your servant, so I suggest you get yourself a basket from that pile over there and start filling."

I scanned the nearest shelf for the first item on my list: pork and beans. It took me three wall-to-wall searches before I found a can nestled between boxes of cereal and bread. Next up was toilet paper, found under the daily newspaper. Band-aids—where had I seen them? Oh, yes, next to the face cream. The store was a puzzle, but it held some surprises, too. I found a new Superman comic tucked behind the peanut butter.

I visited Miss Bee a couple of times a week that summer. Sometimes she short-changed me. Other times she overcharged. Or sold me an old newspaper instead of one that was current. Going to the store was more like going into battle. I left my Grandma's house with my list and marched into Miss Bee's.

"That can of beans is only twenty-nine cents!" I corrected her one afternoon. I had watched the numbers change on the cash register closely, and Miss Bee had added 35 cents. She didn't seem embarrassed that I had caught her overcharging. She just looked at me over her glasses and corrected the price.

Not that she ever let me declare victory. All summer long she found ways to trip me up. No sooner had I learned how to pronounce bicarbonate of soda and memorized its location on the shelf, than Miss Bee rearranged the shelves and made me hunt for it all over again. By summer's end the shopping trip that had once taken me an hour was done in 15 minutes. The morning I was to return to Brooklyn, I stopped in to get a packet of gum.

"All right, Miss Potential," she said. "What did you learn this summer?"

"That you're a meany!" I said.

To my amazement, Miss Bee laughed. "I know what you think of me," she said. "Well, here's a news flash: I don't care! Each of us is put on this earth for a reason. I believe my job is to teach every child I meet ten life lessons to help them. Think what you will, Miss Potential, but when you get older you'll be glad our paths crossed!" Glad I met Miss Bee? Ha! The idea was absurd...

Until one day my daughter came to me with homework troubles.

"It's too hard," she said. "Could you finish my math problems for me?"

"If I do it for you how will you ever learn to do it yourself?" I said. Suddenly, I was back at that general store where I had learned the hard way to tally up my bill along with the cashier. Had I ever been overcharged since?

As my daughter went back to her homework, I wondered: had Miss Bee really taught me something all those years ago? I took out some scrap paper and started writing.

Sure enough, I had learned ten life lessons:

1. Listen well.

2. Never assume—things aren't always the same as they were yesterday.

3. Life is full of surprises.

4. Speak up and ask questions.

5. Don't expect to be bailed out of a predicament.

6. Everyone isn't as honest as I try to be.

7. Don't be so quick to judge other people.

8. Try my best, even when the task seems beyond me.

9. Double-check everything.

10. The best teachers aren't only in school.

无论何时只要你感到快乐，你就吸收了营养。

——爱默生

到肉铺买肉、去食品杂货店买食品，这都很平常。可那年夏天我待在奶奶家时，她写了一张购物清单叫我到一家杂货店买东西。我又怎么可能在杂货店的横七竖八的货架上找到我想要买的商品呢？

我走近柜台。柜台后面有一位我从未见过如此长相的女人。

"打扰一下。"我说。女人抬起了头。

"你就是克莱门特家的小孩吧，"她说。"我是蜜蜂小姐。过来让我好好看看。"蜜蜂小姐把眼镜向鼻子上扶了扶说道："如果商店失窃，我好向治安官描述你的外貌特征。"

"我又不是小偷！"我有些吃惊。我才7岁啊！怎么可能当小偷呢！

"在我看来，你只是个黄毛丫头。我觉得你有这方面的潜质。"

"我要买这些东西。"我说着，举起手里的购物单给她看。

"那又怎样？去取啊。"蜜蜂小姐用手指了一下纱门上的一块牌子。"这里就我们俩，我不是你的佣人，所以我建议你最好到那一摞篮子那儿拿一个，找到要买的东西就往里面放。"

我从离我最近的货架开始逐层寻找购物单上第一件商品:猪肉和豆子。我来来回回找了三次，才在一堆面包和麦片里发现一听猪肉。第二件是一卷手纸，在一份新闻报纸下找到的。这家商店就像一座迷宫，然而里面却充满惊喜。我在花生酱后面还发现一本新的超人漫画!

那年夏天，我每个星期都要到蜜蜂小姐的店铺几趟。有时，蜜蜂小姐少收我钱；有时，她多收我钱。更甚的是，她还把前一天的报纸当作当天的报纸卖给我。我到她店里买东西，感觉就像上战场一样。带着购物单我离开奶奶家向蜜蜂小姐的杂货店挺进。

"那听豆子只要29美分。"一天下午，我纠正蜜蜂小姐道。我紧盯着收款机上的数字变化，蜜蜂小姐入账时记的是35美分。被我察觉多收了钱后，蜜蜂小姐毫无难堪之色。她越过镜框瞥了我一眼，然

后把价格改了过
来。

她从不让我宣
告胜利。整个夏
天，她想尽办法来
捉弄我。我刚记住
小苏打的发音以及
它在货架上的位
置，她就调整了
商品的排列，害
得我又一顿好找。暑假快结束了，以前耗时要一小时的购物之行，
现在15分钟就完事了。在我要返回布鲁克林的那天早上，我到蜜蜂
小姐杂货店买一包口香糖。

"好了，潜能小姐，"她说，"这个夏天你都学到了什么？"

"你是个十分刻薄的人！"

令人惊奇的是，蜜蜂小姐大笑起来。"我知道你是怎么看我
的，"她说，"但你不会想到：我并不在意！人生于世，各得其所。
我相信我的任务是教会我遇到的每一位小朋友人生的十个教益。随便
你怎么想，潜能小姐，但当你长大后，就会发现我俩的相遇其实是一
件值得庆幸的事。"庆幸遇见蜜蜂小姐？哈！这想法真是荒唐……

直到有一天，女儿拿着作业来到我的身边。

"这些数学题太难了。你能替我做吗？"她说。

"如果妈妈替你做了，那你自己如何能学会呢？"我说。这时

候，我突然想起那时在蜜蜂小姐杂货店的情景：我吃力地核对着收款机里的数目。自那时起，我有被多收过钱吗？

当我的女儿回过头继续做作业时，我在想：蜜蜂小姐真的在多年前就向我传授了若干人生之道吗？我随手拿起了纸，开始动笔记录。

确实，我学到了整整十条人生教益：

1. 学会仔细倾听。

2. 不要想当然——事物每天都在变化。

3. 生活充满惊喜。

4. 大声说出你的问题。

5. 不要以为身临困境总会有援手。

6. 并不是每一个人都像你一样诚实。

7. 不要急于评判他人。

8. 凡事要竭尽全力，即使任务似乎超出自己的能力范围。

9. 仔细复核每个环节。

10. 最好的老师并不只在学校。

词汇识记

potential [pə'tenʃl] *n.* 潜力，潜能

例：Education develops potential abilities.

教育能开发人的潜能。

absurd [əb'sɜːd] *adj.* 荒唐的，可笑的，不合理的

例：What an absurd suggestion!

多荒谬的建议啊！

assume [ə'sjuːm] *v.* 假定，设想，（想当然的）认为

例：Let's assume it to be true.

让我们假定这是真的。

短语搭配

I visited Miss Bee a couple of times a week that summer.

a couple of: 两个，几个

造句：_____

To my amazement, Miss Bee laughed.

To one's amazement: 使某人惊奇的是

造句：_____

译展身手

人生于世，各得其所。

译：_____

这家商店就像一座迷宫，然而里面却充满惊喜。

译：_____

The Other Woman
第三者

Love consists in this, that two solitudes protect and border and salute each other.

—Rainer Maria Rilke

A little while ago I had to go out with another woman. It was really my wife's idea.

"I know that you love her," she said one day, taking me by surprise.

"But I love you," I protested.

"I know, but you also love her."

The other woman that my wife wanted me to visit was my mother, who had been a widow for 19 years, but the demands of my work and my three children had made it possible to visit her only occasionally.

On that night I called to invite her to go out for dinner and a movie.

"What's wrong? Are you OK?" she asked. My mother is the type of woman who suspects that a late night call or a surprise invitation is a sign of bad news.

On that Friday night, as I drove over to pick her up, I was a bit nervous. When I arrived at her house, I noticed that she seemed to be nervous about our date too. She had curled her hair and was wearing the dress that she had worn to celebrate her last wedding anniversary.

We went to a restaurant that, although not elegant, was very nice and cozy. My mother took my arm as if she were the First Lady. After we sat down, I had to read the menu. Her eyes could only read large print. Half-way through reciting the entries, I lifted my eyes and saw Mom sitting there staring at me. A nostalgic smile was on her lips.

"It was I who used to have to read the menu when you were small," she said.

"Then it's time that you relax and let me return the favor," I responded.

During dinner we had an agreeable conversation —nothing extraordinary—and caught up on recent events of each other's life.

We talked so much that we missed the movie. As we arrived at her house later, she said, "I'll go out with you again, but only if you let me invite you."

A few days later my mother died of a massive heart attack. It happened so suddenly that I didn't have a chance to do anything for her.

Some time later I received an envelope with a copy of a restaurant receipt from the same place where my mother and I had dined. An attached note said, "I paid this bill in advance. I was almost sure that I couldn't be there; nevertheless, I paid for two plates—one for you and the other for your wife. You will never know what that night meant for me. I love you."

At that moment I understood the importance of saying in time: "I LOVE YOU" and giving our loved ones the time that they deserve. Nothing in life is more important than your family. Give them the time they deserve. Love cannot be put off till some other time.

两颗寂寞的心相爱护、相偎依、相敬重，爱就在此间。

　　　　　　　　　　　——赖内·马利亚·里尔克

　　前不久，我奉妻子之命，不得不跟另一个女人出去"约会"了。

　　某天，妻子说："我知道你爱她。"这着实让我吃了一惊。

　　我争辩道："但是我爱你。"

　　"我知道，但你也爱她。"

　　妻子让我去拜访的"第三者"正是我已经守寡了19年的妈妈，工作加上三个孩子所带来的劳累和繁琐，让我几乎没有时间去看她，除了偶尔几次。

　　那天晚上，我打电话邀请她外出晚餐和看电影。

　　妈妈问我："怎么了？你还好吧？"深夜的电话或意外的拜访，妈妈都会疑心是不好的兆头。

　　那个星期五晚上，开车去接她时，我竟然有点紧张。到了妈妈家，我注意到她似乎也对我们的"约会"感到紧张。显然她事先把头发烫卷了，还把她在最后一个结婚纪念日穿的衣服穿上了。

　　我们去了一家算不上雅致但是很干净、很温馨的餐馆。妈妈把手搭在我的臂弯，似乎她就是第一夫人。坐下后，由于妈妈只能看清大号字，所以由我来读菜单。在给妈妈念菜单的中途，我抬眼，看见妈妈正盯着我看，嘴角挂着怀旧的微笑。

她说道："你小的时候，读菜单的人通常都是我。"

我回答："那么现在您该放松放松，由我来为您效劳了。"

晚餐期间，我们说了说各自的近况，没有什么特别的事，但是交谈非常愉快。

要说的太多了，我们竟然错过了电影。后来，回到她的住处时，她说道："如果你同意的话，我会邀请你，咱们再去'约会'。"

几天后，妈妈由于严重的心脏病去世了。事情太突然，我什么都来不及为她做。

过了一段时间，我收到了我和妈妈曾经共进晚餐的那家餐馆寄来的一封信，里面是一张餐馆收据的复印件。附上的留言写着："我已经预先付款了。我几乎可以肯定自己不能再到那里了；但是，我订了两个人的座位——给你和你的妻子。你永远不会明白那天晚上对我有多么重要。我爱你。"

那一刻，我明白了及时说出"我爱你"和给予你爱的人他们应得的时间有多么重要。生活中没有比家庭更重要的了。给予家人应得的时间。爱不能被拖到"下次再说"。

词汇识记

protest ['prəʊtest] *v.* 抗议，反对

例：They protested to the mayor that the taxes were too high.

他们向市长提出抗议说税款过高。

suspect [səs'pekt] *v.* 怀疑，猜想

例：I suspect he was lying by the boy's abnormal behaviour.

从那个男孩的反常举动中，我怀疑他在撒谎。

relax [rɪ'læks] *v.* 休息，放松，使……放松

例句：The music will help to relax you.

音乐会使你感到轻松。

短语搭配

A few days later my mother died of a massive heart attack.

die of: 死于

造句：_____

I paid this bill in advance.

in advance: 提前，预先

造句：_____

Love cannot be put off till some other time.

put off: 推迟，延迟

造句：_____

译展身手

那天晚上，我打电话邀请她外出晚餐和看电影。

译：_____

生活中没有比家庭更重要的了。

译：_____

Be Yourself and Stay Unique
做最特别的自己

With talent, you do what you like. With genius, you do what you can.

—Jean Ingres

Be yourself and stay unique. Your imperfections make you beautiful, lovable, and valuable.

Memories can make you smile, but it can very well make you cry hard.

Giving up doesn't mean you're weak, sometimes it means you're strong enough to let go.

By desiring little, a poor man makes himself rich.

Heart is a fertile place. Anything planted in it will grow whether it's love or hate.

Life is not measured by the number of breaths we take, but by the moments that take our breath away.

Life is a pure flame, and we live by an invisible sun within us.

It's not easy to change friendship into love. But it's even harder to turn love into friendship.

Life can only be understood backwards, but it must be lived forwards.

As long as you are still alive, you will definitely encounter the good things in life.

Concentrate on what you have, instead of wishing for what you don't have.

Love makes time pass, time makes love pass.

Love does not consist in gazing at each other, but in looking outward together in the same direction.

My interest is in the future because I am going to spend the rest of my life there.

Sometimes you need patience in order to find true happiness. It won't come fast and it won't come easy, but it will be worth it.

The dream was always running ahead of me. To catch up, to live for a moment in unison with it, that was the miracle.

Save your heart for someone who cares.

Everyday starts with some expectations but ends with some experiences.

When the world says, "Give Up!" Hope whispers, "Try it one more time."

Wherever you go, no matter what the weather, always bring your own sunshine.

有才能的人，做自己喜爱的事；有天赋的人，做自己能做的事。

——让·安格尔

做最特别的自己。正因为你的不完美，你才如此美丽、可爱、珍贵！

回忆有时令你嘴角上扬，但有时也能让你潸然泪下。

放弃并不总意味着软弱，有时反而说明你足够坚强去舍弃。

奢求少一点，穷人也会变成富人。

人的内心是一块肥沃的土壤。无论种下的是爱或是恨，都能在这里茁壮成长。

生命的质量不是在于你活了多久，而是那些令人怦然心动的精彩瞬间。

生命如纯洁的火焰，而维系这火焰的是我们内心的太阳。

让友情变成爱情不是件容易的事，而让爱情变成友情却更难。

要理解生活，需要往后看；要过好生活，必须往前看。

只要活着一定会遇上好事的。

珍惜你现在拥有的，而不是期待自己没有的。

爱情让时间匆匆而过，时间让爱情消逝于无形。

爱不在于彼此凝视，而在于注视着同一个方向。

我只关心未来，因为我的余生都会在那里度过。

很多时候，为了求得真正的幸福，我们需要保持耐心。因为真正的幸福不会很快到来，也不会轻易到来，但它值得等待。

梦想总是跑在我的前面。努力追寻它们，为了那一瞬间的同步，这就是动人的生命奇迹。

为了某个在乎你的人，请节约你的真心！

每一天都以许下希望开始，以收获经验结束。

当全世界都要我放弃，还是期待有人轻语一声：再试一次！

无论去哪儿，什么天气，记得带上自己的阳光。

词汇识记

unique [juːˈniːk] *adj.* 独特的，独一无二的，稀罕的

例：Her style of writing is rather unique.

她的写作风格很不寻常。

measure [ˈmeʒə(r)] *v.* 测量，比较，权衡

例：He measured the length of the room.

他量了房间的长度。

encounter [ɪnˈkaʊntə(r)] *v.* 遭遇，遇到，偶然碰到

例：I encountered an old friend at Rome.

我在罗马邂逅了一个老朋友。

patience ['peɪʃns] *n*. 耐心，忍耐，毅力
例：Learning to walk again after his accident required great patience.
他出事后重新学习走路要有极大的毅力。

短语搭配

Giving up doesn't mean you're weak, sometimes it means you're strong enough to let go.

give up: 放弃

造句：_____

As long as you are still alive, you will definitely encounter the good things in life.

as long as: 只要

造句：_____

My interest is in the future because I am going to spend the rest of my life there.

in the future: 未来；往后；将来

造句：_____

译展身手

珍惜你现在拥有的，而不是期待自己没有的。

译：_____

很多时候，为了求得真正的幸福，我们需要保持耐心。

译：_____

声　明

本书的选编，我们选用了大量的文章，获得了广大读者、作者的
支持和帮助，在此，我们深表谢意。但是，由于作者面广，时间
跨度大，尽管我们多方努力，还是与一部分作者（译者）未能取
得联系，谨致深深的歉意。敬请原作者（译者）或著作权人见到
书后，及时与我们联系，以便我们按国家有关规定支付稿酬并赠
送样书。

联 系 人：王老师　　联系电话：010-85866269

电子邮箱：huanyuhongji@vip.sina.com

图书在版编目（CIP）数据

美国语文拓展阅读系列．妙语名篇．心灵的塑造：
英文／尹燕燕主编．－－北京：北京联合出版公司，
2017.5
　　ISBN 978-7-5596-0057-8

Ⅰ．①美… Ⅱ．①尹… Ⅲ．①英语－阅读教学－自学
参考资料 Ⅳ．①H319.4

中国版本图书馆CIP数据核字(2017)第068054号

妙语名篇
心灵的塑造

选题策划：益博轩
主　　编：尹燕燕
责任编辑：谢晗曦　夏应鹏

北京联合出版公司出版
（北京市西城区德外大街83号楼9层　　100088）
北京富达印务有限公司印刷　新华书店经销
字数140千字　880毫米×1230毫米　1/32　7印张
2017年5月第1版　2017年5月第1次印刷
ISBN 978-7-5596-0057-8
定价：28.00元